The Cat-Lover's Bedside Book

THE CAT
BEDSIDE

edited by

CAT SHOW

Siamese · Russian · Tabby · Moggie · Domesti...

LOVER'S
BOOK

Grace Pond

B. T. BATSFORD LTD
London

First published 1974

© B. T. Batsford Ltd 1974

ISBN 0 7134 2802 3

Made and printed in Great Britain by
Bristol Typesetting Co Ltd
Barton Manor, St Philips, Bristol
for the publishers B. T. Batsford Ltd
4 Fitzhardinge Street, London W1H 0AH

Contents

The Contributors

JANE ANTHONY
Writer and Advisor on Animal Welfare, *Woman*

ALISON ASHFORD
International Cat Judge and Breeder

JANET COATES BARBER
World Wild Life Fund

MARY BATTEN
Siamese cat breeder. All Breeds Judge Australia

PETER BLACK
Journalist and Critic *Daily Mail*

JOHN BOWER, BVSC., MRCVS
Veterinary Surgeon

JOHN CRAIG
Writer *Daily Express*

ANNE CUMBERS
Animal Photographer

A. A. DAMSTEEG
International Cat judge and Breeder Holland

GRAHAME DANGERFIELD
Naturalist and Broadcaster

MARY DUNNILL
Secretary to Siamese Cat Club and Breeder

MAY EUSTACE
Author, International Cat judge and breeder

EDNA M. FIELD
International Cat Judge and breeder Canada and USA

MARGARET COOPER GAY
Author

ALETHA HENDRICKSON
Breeder Angora cats

PHYLLIS LAUDER
Author, International Cat judge and breeder.

BERNARD LEVIN
Journalist, Critic and Broadcaster

COMPTON MACKENZIE
Author and Broadcaster

CHRISTINE METCALF
Writer on Cats

M. OLDFIELD HOWEY
Author

GRACE POND
Author, International cat judge and breeder

ANGELA SAYER
Cat breeder of Foreign and new varieties

MICHAEL SAYER
Owner Boarding Cattery and Kennels

BLANCHE AND RAYMOND SMITH
Cat breeders, Writers and Publishers, USA

WALDO CARLTON WRIGHT
Writer USA

KIT WILSON
Late International Cat Judge and Author

MICHAEL WILSON
Art Expert, Victoria & Albert Museum London

The Illustrations

Acknowledgments

The editor and publishers wish to thank the following for permission to include the passages and quotations acknowledged below (page references are to *The Cat-Lover's Bedside Book*): poems by Jane Anthony (pages 66 and 84) from *Woman*, June 1955 and September 1956; Peter Black, ' Elegant Alice, (pages 28-30) from *Daily Mail*; Thurlow Craig, ' Our wild, hungry Irish Cat ' (pages 39-40) from *Sunday Express*; Margaret Cooper Gay, ' The fundamentals of social hygiene, (pages 140-3) *How to live with a Cat'* (Reinhardt & Evans, 1949); A. A. Damsteeg, ' An Abyssinian over eighty years old ' (pages 171-3) from *Our Cats* July 1961; quotation from Sidney and Helen Denham, *The Siamese Cat* (page 73); Gilean Douglas, ' Cats in our language ' (pages 38, 59, 98, 109, 139, 176, 197) from *Our Cats*, November 1957 M. Oldfield Howey, ' The evil spirit and the mummified cat ' (pages 174-6) from *The Cat in Mysteries of Religion and Magic* (Rider and Co., 1930); Bernard Levin, ' The lives and times of Smoky Dostoievski, and others (pages 15-8) from *The Times*, 13th February 1973; Compton Mackenzie, ' No cats about the house ' (pages 101-9) from *Cat's Company* (Elek Books, 1960); Waldo Carlton Wright, ' Feline flood rescues ' (pages 193-7) from *Cats Magazine*, December 1972.

Acknowledgment is also due to Bruce Angrave and *Woman* for the cartoon on page II, to Peter Dennis for the text decorations, and to the following for the photographs appearing in the book: Albert E. Allen for page 49 (bottom); Anne Cumbers for pages 16, 17, 49 (top), 64, 65, 81, 96, 97, 112, 113, 128, 129 (both), 144, 145, 160 and 192; A. A. Damsteeg for page 176 (bottom); Kenneth Scoven for page 161; Sally Anne Thompson and Animal Photography Ltd for pages 32, 33, 48, 80 and 193 (both); Trustees of the Victoria and Albert Museum for page 172 (both).

I

Cats of Character

The lives and times of
Smoky Dostoievski and others

BERNARD LEVIN

This year's champion dog at Cruft's, I see, is called Alansmere Aquarius, and if you think that that is sufficient burden for a particularly soppy-looking spaniel to bear, I can only say that it is mild by the usual standards, previous winners having been called things like Le Vicomte de Fichemoy-Lapaix with Mercury in the Ascendant, or Pride of Tralee (neé Treppengeländer) the Third. Mind you, if you think that dogs (revolting creatures one and all, which deserve no better) are alone in the business of having names above their station, I must reveal that cats themselves are not immune, as an experience of mine a few years ago showed me with embarrassing clarity.

I was seeking a birthday present for my redheaded god-daughter, and had determined upon a kitten. (I have always followed the principle that you may give a child almost anything, even a musical instrument, without asking the parents, but not a pet, on which the elders have a right to be consulted, and I added toolkits to the rule after an unfortunate experience with a young friend to whom I had presented one on his birthday with a breezy suggestion that he was now perfectly equipped to saw one leg off the dining-room table, only to discover half an hour later that he had entirely missed the note of facetiousness in my voice, and was happily engaged in carrying out my suggestion.)

I went to Harrods pet department, which is really a small zoo, and there had to resist, as I always have to, the temptation to ask for a ring-tailed malagazook (this was an enchanting though mythical furry creature rather like a large squirrel, which figured in a strip cartoon I followed in my childhood, its name being Muriel and its usual companions a bear called Happy and a tortoise named Oswald). Instead, I demanded a kitten, and was shown a group of the most exquisite Russian blues. I picked the most exquisite of all, and ordered it wrapped in a comfortable carrying basket. What I had forgotten was the pedigree, at the sight of which the entire enterprise very nearly foundered, for apart from being some nine or ten times the length of the creature it referred to, it disclosed that the name of the kitten was, so help me, Ruchotski Dostoievski, and the contrast between this nonsense and the thing purring in the crook of my arm was so great that I burst on the instant into screams of laughter, heedless of the danger that if Mr John Aspinall had been passing through the store at that moment he would have bought me on the spot as a hyena and added me to his collection.

Anyway, though Mr Aspinall was not present, the Harrods staff were, and were so shocked at this act of *lèse*-ancestry that I really thought they were going to refuse to sell me the kitten on the grounds that I was not a fit and proper person to buy it. Nor did my appeal to them to envisage my redheaded friend going to the back door and calling 'Ruchotski Dostoievski, Ruchotski Dostoievski, come and have your milk' go down much better.

Well, I made my getaway, and next day the kitten was handed over and duly fallen in love with. When I produced the pedigree, however, there was general agreement that some abbreviation of Ruchotski Dostoievski was clearly called for, and after a brief discussion over tea the kitten was rechristened Smoky, which it remains to this day, having in the meanwhile grown a great deal larger and even more beautiful—which could also, it occurs to me, be said of my redheaded god-daughter.

'I wish the photographer would hurry up'.
Red point Colourpoint kitten

Longhaired Red Tabby nodding off in the sun

Later, a puppy was introduced into the family, a present (not from me) for the redhead's brother, and was instantly christened Tolstoy. The introduction of Smoky (who by then had firmly taken over the household) to the newcomer was expected to pose problems. They were brought together in a gingerly fashion, and put down face to face. Smoky first stared at the eager, friendly little dog with a look of stupefaction mingled with contempt. He then walked carefully right round Tolstoy, inspecting him from every angle, then returned to the front end and did something which until then I would have sworn could only happen in a Tom and Jerry cartoon: he raised his right front paw and cracked Tolstoy across the face with it like an old-fashioned girl receiving an improper suggestion. Thereafter they became firm friends, and remained so until Tolstoy's untimely death, but from that moment there was never any doubt who was in charge.

Smoky, however, is far from the most extraordinary cat that has ever passed through my life, though it would be hard to say which one deserves that particular title. The first, which still, more than a third of a century later, remains the noblest and handsomest cat I have ever known, was called Tim; he was a magnificent Persian, who could hear the cat's-meat man coming down the street long before we could, and who used to sleep in the shop window, thus ensuring that, not less often than once a month, a passer-by would enter to inquire, sometimes having struck a bet on the point with a companion, whether this wonderful creature was real or stuffed, at which my grandfather would call 'Tim!', and Tim (who did not, of course, need the cue, knowing perfectly well what the visitor wanted to know) would leap from the window and rub himself up against the inquirer's legs.

Tim lived to an immense age, surviving countless hazards such as being frozen solid one winter's night when he wouldn't come in, and even being poisoned by a neighbour; his predecessor died badly, after falling into a pot of paint, and so did his successor, a lean, glossy, black one who was hit by a car and had a leg unsplintably broken.

Then, after a few unmemorable ones, and one which was memorable for the fact that it was afraid of mice, came the one which never had a name at all, being addressed simply as 'Cat'. (Old Possum, of course, pointed out that

> *The Naming of Cats is a difficult matter,*
> *It isn't just one of your holiday games;*

B

You may think at first I'm as mad as a hatter
When I tell you, a cat must have
THREE DIFFERENT NAMES.)

Cat arrived one day on the doorstep, only about four inches long, and his face lopsided from a kick. Since no cat has ever been turned away from any doorstep beyond which I or any member of my family lives, he was taken in and fed and, knowing a good thing when he saw one, announced that he was going to remain (he did this by crawling under the stove and flatly refusing to come out for three days). Unfortunately, the kick had permanently disfigured him, and his face never grew straight again. This did not seem to worry him at all, though he looked bizarre, as a great length of pink tongue always hung, unretractably, from the corner of his mouth. One day, sleeping in the sun over the porch, he rolled off and fell to the ground, landing on his head and biting off the surplus tongue. To our astonishment, all he did was to unroll a fresh length, which protruded as far as before, though the end of it was now concave in shape.

Cat, incidentally, later on fell from a windowledge two storeys up, and survived even that, though I think he was never quite right in the head thereafter. Later still, he developed some problem with his jaw, as well he might, and was in great pain; we suggested having him put to sleep, but the vet would not hear of it, briskly saying that all he needed was to have his teeth out. Out they came, and he was as fit as ten immediately, though the fact that the two canine teeth had been left, combined with his by now very irregularly shaped face, made him look like a feline Dracula. He never seemed to have any trouble eating, though he never learnt the trick of doing so with his paw like the one in the television advertisement. Cat died of a fit.

Nowadays I live in a flat too high, and am out of it too much, to keep a cat, for cats, despite all their marvellous self-sufficiency and independence, do not like being alone, especially without being able to come and go at will. Below me there lives a corgi, with which I have established a kind of armed neutrality; a friend of mine dubbed it Baskerville, and it is as Baskerville that I always think of it. It could eat Alansmere Aquarius alive, though it wouldn't have gone three rounds against Cat, let alone Ruchotski Dostoievski. But I shall dream of Tim tonight.

Cats of my childhood

MAY EUSTACE

The nostalgic longings for childhood days superimposes itself on
everything I write.

> *Why do I write,*
> *What sin to me unknown,*
> *Dipt me in ink,*
> *My parents' or my own?*
> Alexander Pope

Looking back on my yesterdays is to me an exercise in solace and
inspiration. No other human experience fills me with such delight.
When I reminisce I forget all the cares of the world. I forget that
I am getting old. I forget that I am now nearly altogether alone.
I forget that I have tax forms to fill in and pension books to sign.
I forget all the irritations of the present and enjoy again the old

familiar haunts, with the old folks and the animals who first taught me how to live.

> *I remember, I remember,*
> *The house where I was born,*
> *The little windows where the sun,*
> *Came peeping in at dawn.*

Yes, those were the days. Clearly as through a looking glass I see the old home, the gardens, the paddocks and rivulets. And I see the pathways, too, which leads to the river and the woods carpeted with bluebells, primroses and cowslips. And then—as if I ever could forget—I see my mother and father again. Mother's long black skirt is trailing in the dust and my father's moustache seems longer and bushier than before. They are still speaking in whispers, as if they still have some unfinished business in hand. It was the business of love and sex. Our family was not yet complete.

And, fortunately for us children our parents were so taken up with each other for they left us very much to our own devices. Within reason we could do what we liked. The same good fortune followed the cats. They were everywhere, males and females together, just living their own lives in their own sweet ways. I know that mother never had a kitten destroyed and there were many of them coming and going in all directions. If I had today's official standards of points I am sure I would have found amongst them Rexes and Havanas, Silver Tabbies and British Blues and Bi-coloureds galore.

I was only a small child when the seeds of cat enchantment were sown within me. Not in a namby-pamby way but in a studious and interested fashion more becoming to an older child. And I repeat again that cats were everywhere. On a sunny day they came out in number, each selecting its very own sheltered and sunny spot. Ostensibly none of these outdoor cats could claim from us a roof for their heads. We had our own recognised cat dynasty, which included Rosey, our old housekeeper's cat and one or two others who scrounged their own kind of living. But we had plenty of surplus rations which we handed out freely to the strays.

But how many of these multi-coloured or self-coloured cats were really strays? There was one little tabby who always had her afternoon nap on my window sill. She basked in the sunshine like an oriental goddess. She felt and smelled good. Her ears stood up sharply and she had wisdom written all over her little

striped face. She had a cute black nose which seemed to direct her
always to the sun. I would not say that she was an over-friendly
cat. She did not permit too many familiarities—one or two little
rubs, a tickle under her chin, a gentle touch to her little thick tail.
No more. She let me know she did not like my overtures and stood
up and went away. I thought that an apt name for her would be
Winny Silly.

Our next sunbather was the doorstep cat. He was pure black
and every inch a male. I was sure of this because I often heard
Rosey using bad language towards him; nevertheless he sat it out
though his noxious presence angered the humans. He was quite
an agreeable old fellow and permitted me to rub him down and
tickle his chin. We called him Steptoe, not after the TV character
we know today, but because of his location preference and also
after our uncle. He was a very rich farmer and came to Kilkenny
once a year. He did not trust anyone to do his buying and selling
and when he came down the road on a fair day he had the biggest
herd of cattle of all the farmers. He specialised in the Hertford-
shires and congratulated himself on being a quality breeder. He
had only one weakness: he always celebrated a good sale with a
good drink. He liked his whisky neat and always ordered it in
doubles. Mother did not seem to mind for she said it was his own
money he spent and he could do what he liked with it—his pockets
always bulged with £5 and £10 notes. When my father helped
him into his cart he just dropped down in the straw like an
asphyxiated pig and the pony went along home without any
direction, keeping to his own side of the road and negotiating his
entrance to the drive carefully.

But Steptoe held onto the step no matter who was coming and
going, so long as it was sunny and warm. You were at liberty to
step over him but not to displace him.

The barn cat was a black and white one and the most determined sunbather of the lot. He was not so distinguished-looking
as Steptoe. His coat was rather coarse, there were odd smudges of
white on his tummy and the tip of his tail was white for a good
half-inch. He was domesticated too and never objected to having
his whiskers pulled. Like the others, whose names were associated
with their own selected habitat, we found that Barny was a
heaven-ordained name for him. He always hung round the barn
and it would appear that he had a special friendship for the little
black Kerry cow who was house-bound until her calf was born. She

was known to wander and had her calves in the most unlikely places. Once she actually gave birth while standing in a stream. Only by the merest fluke was she found in time. In the meantime, if the sun shone, Barny came out to enjoy it and if the weather was bad he went into the straw with the cow. Sometimes we did not see him round for a couple of weeks. He did not smell so much of cat as of cow dung.

With regard to smells and scents country folk are more discriminating than those born in towns. The scents of lilacs and roses could never obliterate the smells associated with animals. But Rosey had a town nose really and particularly disliked tom-cat odour. If she got the slightest whiff she was away for the dog or for her switch.

Then there was the most beautiful of all the cats—the white Persian. I say 'beautiful', but I ought to have said 'could have been beautiful' for her coat was always very dirty. Her lovely fan-like tail was trailed in the dirt too. I am absolutely certain that she had blue eyes which she used to advantage—if ever a cat winked an acknowledgment it was Persi. Her favourite haunt was the stable where we kept the big brown stallion. He was an enormous fellow and generated a special kind of heat which appealed to cats. Persi did not have to cuddle up to him; you could always see the perspiration coming from his body. Though he was a noble beast, full of puissance and fertility, the occasion for him to prove himself never arose.

Besides those named there were also more cats hiding in the hay lofts and it only needed the sun to bring them out. It was interesting to see how the various cats reacted to weather changes. I do not know what Kilkenny weather is like now but I remember half a century ago it was always raining. My mother pointed out that the ever-green grass and the lush vegetation everywhere was the result of the pleasant moist climate. She loved the rain. Once she went on a holiday to her brother in Wembley and she said the weather was too clammy and dry; she longed for the drip, drip, drip, that seemed to be going on forever round our old home. I can remember standing so often in the porch waiting for the sun to shine and my pal and I chanted the popular dirge 'Rain, rain, go to Spain, and never come back again'. During these wet periods the cats disappeared altogether. All, of course, except our own cats who had managed to sequester themselves in some quiet corners. But no stray cats were allowed the comfort of Rosey's kitchen. She did not keep her hearth so beautifully polished and the surrounding brasses so exquisitely radiant and shining to dazzle the eyes of the strays. This inviting spot was hers and for her little cat alone. Even the house dogs on the payroll were not encouraged to loiter in the comforting glow from the turf fire and the logs.

It was really Nan that set our project in action. Nan was one of the songsters who was with me singing in the rain. She was also one of my best school friends and had a big heart for all cats.

'Where is Winny Silly today?' she asked, seeing the vacant corner.

'Funny you should ask as I was just wondering the same myself. Every time it rains she goes away. Suppose we try to find out where her second home is?' I replied.

'Yes,' said Nan, 'we will run after her next time she comes and decides to leave.'

'And there are others, too, who sit around in the sun for days at a time and as soon as the weather breaks—away they go. It would be fun to find out where they all live.' And there and then we embarked on a project which would establish for all time the true homes of all our visiting felines.

It was quite a few days before we could get our plan started. The weather had been most inviting and we saw all the cats in their sunbathing haunts. I told Nan that mother had prophesied that the low clouds now in the sky meant that rain was on the way. And she was right. Nan had barely arrived when the first drops fell. The first to really get the message was Winny Silly. She was away in a flash with the two of us after her. She jumped over the garden gate like a born athlete, wound her way along the hedge, through the woodside, in and out amongst the trees. We were both out of breath trying to keep up with her. To make matters worse Nan fell down a marshy slope and commenced to cry, 'I think I will go home. We'll never catch her, and I am so tired.'

But I dismissed her complaints and she soon stopped them and came running on with the same zest as she had at the start. We had Winny in sight when she took a sharp turn into the lane leading to the priest's house. We watched her let herself in through the window with such aplomb that we knew she was home. We waited round for a bit and she did not come out. So that was that. Our first query was solved: Winny Silly was the priest's cat. Sunbathing on my windowsill meant nothing to her. She was there because she liked the shelter it afforded her. She had no love for stray humans. When life suddenly became hard, and the cruel winds of winter buffeted her about, she knew where she could find comfort—on the welcoming knees of the priest's housekeeper. Here food was plentiful and warmth abundant.

Finding Steptoe's domicile took a more exhaustive search. In the first place a few drops of rain were not enough to displace him. We watched him while he crouched miserably against the wall, while the rain lashed all about him.

'Come on Nan,' I whispered, 'I think he has had enough.' Yes. That was so. He was moving. First he looked appealingly into Rosey's kitchen. The fire was sending out rays of warmth and light which made Steptoe's skin tickle in anticipation. But before as he had as much as put a foot forward Rosey was after him like a ton of bricks.

'No stray cats here, please!' said Rosey in a language that Steptoe understood. He walked sulkily away. We wore heavy rain wear and wellington boots and continued in Steptoe's wake. Once again he took the same route as Winny, but this time he passed the priest's house and went in the direction of the river. It was like a funeral march for, rain or no rain, Steptoe was in no hurry. He stopped several times for a smell of this and that. Then, quite unexpectedly, he stood in front of his own halldoor but this time is was not the usual kind of door—it was a door that one had to jump over and this abode was a houseboat of sorts. There didn't seem to be any welcoming hands coming out to fondle him; nevertheless he climbed into the cabin, displaying a proprietorial air, and sat himself down. It was evident that this was his real home. No matter how desolate and dreary everything looked in the rain, we were satisfied that this was where Steptoe lived. Later mother told us that an old fellow known as Joxer had laid claim to the boat after the death of the real owner. He was known to be respectable and did odd jobs for the farmers. He did quite a good bit of fishing too and if anyone wanted a nice fresh trout Joxer was their man.

We were very pleased to have found Steptoe's home. Now we had traced back two of our sunbathers. After that I often purloined some of Rosey's cat food for poor Steptoe because I felt he had a lean time on the boat. Miss Winny Silly needed no extra rations for she lived the life of a lady when she was not on our windowsill. She was well fed and well nourished from the generous table of the fat parish priest.

Now for Barny. His conduct was not always predictable. Sometimes for days he disappeared and then we saw him surreptitiously climb through the window of the cow shed. It was certain there was some sort of affinity between the little Kerry cow and him. When we did approach him he was always amiable and we were sure that he was not an abandoned stray. He was never ravenously hungry like Steptoe, so Nan and I agreed that he came from a good home. Yet we had not a single clue. Finding his home would be a hit or miss matter. Unlike Winny and Steptoe he was not driven away by the rain. When his sunbathing was disturbed he just went inside and played the waiting game with the little cow. He lay comfortably in the straw as if time did not matter. Nan and I decided that all we could do was wait. Surely this was wise, for by waiting we found out all we wanted to know about Barny. We were coming home from school one day when a little fellow called Tommy Dockerty asked us if we would play a game of marbles with him. As we had never before been asked favours from boys we agreed to.

'Hold on a minute,' said Tommy, 'I see Jimmy, our cat, coming home for his dinner.' And at that very moment we looked into the eyes of Cowshed Barny. So that was that, Barny—alias Jimmy—had a good home.

As we walked back Nan and I congratulated ourselves on establishing the real identity of Cat Number Three—Barny of the old barn—a cat who had fallen in love with our little cow.

The fourth cat, the dirty white Persian, was the most difficult of all to trace, for she never left the stable. When she was not sunbathing on the roof she was inside with the big horse. She really was a homeless stray as she never left our yard and she was the one cat that was never missing. She was always hungry and ate ravenously in a manner more becoming to a waif and stray than to her Persian forebears. I could never catch her. Nan and I saw her several times a day and we decided that if we could catch her and clean her up she would gain entry in to any society—and most certainly into Rosey's kitchen. The word 'Persian' was magic.

We told mother of the lovely white cat we saw in the stable and we were sure she was a Persian.

'Persian, indeed.' said mother, 'and how could a Persian cat be turned into a waif or stray?'

So 'Persian indeed' was our most difficult quarry. To trace her was not going to be easy.

About this time Nan and I started our education proper at the convent school. No more frolics with Tommy Dockerty and his kind. Every morning we walked nearly two miles, along footpaths, leafy lanes, through the woods and fields, passing the old church and graveyard, and up the hill to the convent. A little later mother got us our own pony and trap and we took him to school every day. It was very difficult getting permission to tie him up at the back gate and there was one thing we had to promise and that was that we must clean up every evening. The little nun who was in charge of the roses welcomed the good manure we placed so liberally on her rose trees. Driving backwards and forward to school, with a car full of scholars, was amongst the proudest and happiest experiences of my early school life.

And soon, very soon indeed, there occurred the last and final key to our cat project. Reverend Mother's first address to the assembly included a request from pupils to keep an eye out for her own very special white Persian cat, which had been missing for about a month.

'Did you hear that Nan?' I whispered, 'could it possibly be Persi?'

Trembling all over I put my hand up to speak 'Please, Mother, I think I know where there is a white Persian.'

'Speak up child,' was her reply but I was not able to speak any louder and I was summoned to the table.

Then everything changed. Suddenly her voice sounded more kindly and the next thing I knew was that I was being sent home with big Alice the convent cook. Yes, she immediately identified Fluffie, the convent cat. While the chase was on she told mother that she was a very special cat, having been imported (or rather smuggled in) from the home of a viscount in Le Mans—a special gift to Reverend Mother for services rendered to his daughter while boarding in the convent. Then Alice took mother aside and said that being a female she was becoming a real annoyance, especially when the male cat population of the town serenaded her all night. It took quite a little while to catch Fluffie as her month's freedom and life as a waif and stray had whetted her appetite for adventure. With the whole of our working staff guarding every exit from the stable, Alice dived headlong under the horse's belly and emerged with a much-bedraggled Fluffie.

Instead of settling down to be the angelic, white-robed creature she used to be, her stay in the outside world had unsettled her. She was no longer content to listen quietly to the angelus bells and the clanking of the rosary beads as the nuns came and went from their devotions. Celibate and happy though her owners might be Fluffie was now rebellious. The quiet of the convent was shaken. After a serious conference in the community it was decided that Fluffie would have to move on—not as a horse's mate in a dull and depressing stable but as a companion for someone of importance in the town.

When Reverend Mother's wishes were made public the convent bell rang loud and often as hopeful hearts sought ownership of the most important cat in town. From several applicants Fluffie was presented to the mayor, for who better than the first citizen to win such a prize?

But now the real fun started. On the night of arrival Fluffie escaped up the chimney and it looked as if she would be impossible to catch, so the First Lady sent out a series of soss. The mayor himself was quickly on the scene and when he looked up the chimney was soon blinded by soot that had been displaced by the cat. More and more soss to civic dignitaries and others. The district nurse outran the doctor and arrived in time to shout: 'Oh, your Lordship! Your poor, dear Lordship! Water, soap, castor oil and brandy! Quick!'

It did not take Ellen, the district nurse, many minutes to get things under control. She cleaned up the mayor, cheered up the mayoress, nipped the wee brandy and went after the cat. By this time Fluffie was in a more agreeable mood and was not so difficult to catch.

'You may take her if you want,' stammered the mayor, 'she is too much for me with my civic duties.'

And so Fluffie became the nurse's cat.

It is so many years ago that I cannot remember all the details but I know that after her weekly bath her coat was as white as snow. She was as sweet as she was handsome—and nurse watched carefully over her morals. The occasional tom who picked up her trail ran for his life if ever he saw nurse appear, so there were never any little Fluffies to carry on the name.

And that was how it was in my youth. Cats and everything to do with them were so much fun.

Elegant Alice

PETER BLACK

The long and fortunate life of our old cat, Alice, has ended at last.

She had reached 21 years and seven months, and had been with us since my wife brought her home in her bicycle basket, eight weeks old. She was an unabashedly ugly kitten with blotchy brown and black markings like a badly cured kipper.

But later she developed into a very neat and attractive kind of tortoiseshell with the standard golden eyes, white feet and stomach and asymmetrical markings of pink and brown down the nose. Her best feature was her tail: to the day of her death it was as large and bushy as a bellrope.

I doubt if any cat had a happier life. We bought her with a tom kitten, named Oscar.

We wanted to try unneutered cats for a change and reasoned—wrongly, of course—that if they had a satisfying relationship at home they wouldn't wander about looking for one.

It was hard on Oscar, who had to fight other toms twice, once in the eliminating bouts as a contending mate and again as defender of his territorial rights.

But Alice thrived on the glamour and excitement of it all and had 42 kittens by 1960, when something went wrong with the delivery service.

Even there she was lucky. Sometimes neutering makes an adult female jumpy and uncertain-tempered. She only put back a bit of flesh. She always insisted on my wife's company when she was having her kittens. She gave birth deftly, confidently, absorbed purring loudly all the time.

It was awesome to watch her instinct taking care of every stage in the birth and the rearing, as though she were tuned in to instructions of some mysterious source. It even told her what she should bring the kittens to play with.

Of all the cats we've had she embodied most of the qualities I like best about the creatures. She was self-sufficient, stoical, dignified, fastidious (her silent rejection of food more than a day old was icy) and endearingly idiotic.

She had her own way of doing things, and that was that.

She never merely accepted affection. She offered it, by jumping on your lap, or declined it by flattening herself and sliding gracefully from under your hand. She could never bear to be picked up.

In one of my wife's frequent dreams about her she'd gone to stay with some friends of ours called George and Devreux. My wife saw George pick her up and heard Alice say (in her dreams all animals talk) in a furious and disbelieving tone: 'Put me down *at once.*'

The *at once* is a key phrase; it's exactly what she would have said.

That such an elegant little creature had so many kittens (though 42 is far below the average) fascinated visitors, and they couldn't get over her air of total independence, her complete mastery of the trick that cats alone have learned, of accepting all the privileges of pets and retaining, absolutely sharp and ready for use, all the protective instincts of a wild animal.

As cats do, she grew older without apparently ageing and then, almost overnight it seemed, looked an old, old cat.

Three years ago she lost her hearing. I think she enjoyed the peace and quiet as if showing that if you kept on at people long enough they'd respect your wishes.

Towards the end of last year her back legs began to weaken. She seemed to withdraw from us. Most of the time she slept.

We'd always vowed that when she couldn't look after herself we'd have her put down. But when it came to giving the order we couldn't.

She ate too well—like so many old people, she enjoyed her food as if all the pleasures had shrunk to what was on the plate.

We hoped the spark would just dwindle and disappear, but at the last her luck ran out.

We think some animal, probably a fox, got into the garden. Her instinct was always to run away, rather than indoors, when ill or scared.

Some neighbours found her on their lawn 300 yards away, soaked by the wet grass and evidently in shock. It was there that we saw the last of her.

We had lived longer with her than with anyone we've known except each other.

One broiling hot summer's day Charles James Fox and the Prince of Wales were lounging up St James's street, and Fox laid the Prince a wager that he would see more Cats than his Royal Highness during their promenade, although the Prince might choose which side of the street he thought fit. On reaching Piccadilly it turned out that Fox had seen thirteen Cats and the Prince none. The Prince asked for an explanation of this apparent miracle.

'Your Royal Highness' said Fox, 'chose, of course, the shady side of the way as most agreeable. I knew that the sunny side would be left for me, and that Cats prefer the sunshine.'

CHAS. H. ROSS, *The Book of Cats*, 1868

A cat is not a dog—or is he?

JANE ANTHONY

I am not a cat woman. I like dogs, with horses a close second. But there were always cats around the edges of my life, because my grandmother was a dedicated stray-feeder and, in addition to her own cats, there was always a little cat colony in her garden, plus a number of regular visitors who were not really strays but just liked her (and the food she put out) better than anything they had at home.

Strays used to turn up in a sad state—bones sticking through staring fur, bits out of ears, straggly tails, bald patches—and my grandmother would take a shrewd knowledgeable look, announce 'That'll make a lovely cat' and put out another dish.

The funny thing was that they *did* all make lovely cats. Food, love and some ointment that Gran used to make up worked miracles and they turned into sleek handsome creatures. Still, technically, strays, they lived happily in the garden until they died of old age or found new homes that matched up to Gran's high standards.

But I never had a cat of my own—always dogs. Until one night, many years later, when Gran was long dead and the garden a housing estate, my husband rang up and said: 'What about us having a kitten?'

He'd been out, all the afternoon and evening, taking a litter of kittens from a cat sanctuary to the new homes that had been arranged for them. Everyone he called on had been delighted—clean old blankets, saucers of warm milk and ping-pong balls showed the kittens were really wanted and he felt pretty happy and satisfied about the whole thing. But when he got to the last address on his list the luck changed. The door opened a crack, a frightened-looking woman said she was very sorry but they'd changed their minds and decided to have a dog instead, and the door closed. It was ten o'clock at night, and there he was, 30 miles from home, with one kitten surplus to requirements.

So there wasn't really much choice—you can't just dump a small trusting creature. My husband brought the kitten home—it was so tiny it looked like a toy when it sat on his hand—and gave it to me. The little claws dug into my sweater, the little square black head butted me on the chin and a funny little squeaky voice announced it was hungry.

Rex, our king-size Alsatian, heard the noise and wanted to know more about it, so he reared up and put his paws on my shoulders to get a closer look. And before I had time to be scared of what would happen, the kitten had given him a calm appraising look, put out one small white-booted paw, patted him gently on the muzzle and said 'Prrrrrrrmp' which seemed to mean that he liked dogs, especially large Alsatians, and it was very thoughtful of us to have provided one for him.

Rex wasn't our only dog. There was Bess, a black Labrador we'd taken from the BUAV lady in Doncaster, and Tramp, a border terrier who'd been practically dead through malnutrition when my husband found her. I suppose one of the things that would have made me hesitate about taking a kitten—if there had been anything else we could do—had been visions of the dogs with their eyes scratched and the kitten torn to shreds and a general 'cat and dog life' atmosphere in our peaceful home.

But neither the dogs nor the kitten had ever heard any of the

The inscrutable Brown Burmese with eyes of chartreuse yellow

Shorthaired Tabby with friend

'dogs and cats hate each other' propaganda. From the first, there was amiable acceptance. In the end, there was love.

We called the kitten Bing, because he was a relaxed sort of person and sang very nicely (it was a toss up between Bing and Perry) and he settled in so smoothly that it seemed as if we had always had a cat.

While he was small, he slept in a plastic washing-up bowl, lined with an old piece of blanket. But he grew very quickly and my husband made him a smaller edition of the dogs' beds and put it down with the others.

Bess stood and looked at this when it was finished. Then she went to her own bed, picked up her favourite rubber duck, and brought it and put it into Bing's bed.

We took it out. Even though dogs and kitten were friendly, we thought there might be ructions if Bing took over Bess's favourite toy. So we put it back where we thought it belonged.

Bess put it back in Bing's bed.

We put it back into Bess's bed.

Bess put it back into Bing's bed. She also gave my husband—who'd done the actual moving—a sorrowful 'why are men so dim?' look and we got the message and left the rubber duck where it was.

From then on, she ignored the duck. She'd made Bing a present of it and he liked it very much and slept with one paw round it.

The whole kitten-introducing operation went smoothly. Of course, for the first few days we watched very carefully, on the better-safe-than-sorry principle, but we needn't have worried. Never once did the dogs show signs of harming the kitten; never once did the kitten show signs of fear. Perhaps one was the result of the other but if so we couldn't decide which was chicken and which was egg.

But all this time Bing was still a kitten—or rather a fine young cat. It wasn't until later that he became a dog.

And, of course, not all at once.

He started to do doggy things. He drank from their water bowl (even when there was milk down for him), liked a piece of dry dog biscuit to crunch and one day, as we walked across the fields with the dogs, we realised Bing had tagged on. We could just see his tail, like a little black periscope, weaving through the long grass as he brought up the rear. After that, he always came.

We acquired another dog, Shane, who had been kicked into the

C

street, unwanted. A police sergeant's wife picked him up and brought him to us. Shane had been brought up on the 'dogs hate cats' myth and after he got over his first fear and misery, he tried to chase Bing. But it is difficult to chase someone who is not running away, so Shane came to an embarrassed halt; Bing gave him a stern look and told him to stop making a fool of himself and they became friends.

Gradually we realised that Bing was identifying more and more with the dogs. When we called 'Dogs!' for walks or meals, or grooming, or their late-night run, there were always five, not four. 'The little black and white dog', as we started to call him, was right there with the others.

He even wore a collar with a bell on it—to give birds and field-mice a sporting chance—and a medallion with our telephone number, in case he strayed.

The next step was that he joined in the nightly routine of 'treats'. We love our animals but we can be firm about some things and one of our rules is *no begging*. All our dogs have always understood that they don't bother us while we are eating but that something—a small piece of meat or fish or some gravy—will be saved for them. Confident that they wouldn't be forgotten, they soon ceased to take any interest in our dinner, so when we had finished we always called 'treats' and they came from wherever they were lying and lined up, while we doled out the titbits, starting with Rex.

But Bing had never been included in this. We saved him something but it was put into his bowl, for a late-night snack. Until one evening, at the word 'treats' he stood up, decided he was to all intents and purposes a dog, and strolled over to join in. The dogs moved up and made room for him and after that we felt we definitely had five dogs, not four dogs and a cat.

One point of difference remained. We believe in one meal a day for healthy adult dogs. Bing didn't mind this for the other four but he continued to like a light breakfast, a little something at midday, and a good square meal in the evening.

Just like the strays that my grandmother used to feed, Bing 'made a lovely cat'. But not for long. We don't know his history—the litter was dumped anonymously at the cat shelter, so there is no knowing what hardship or malnutrition his mother went through, or where or how Bing spent the first few days of his life. He may have been descended from generations of bomb-site cats, ill-fed and often diseased. By the time Bing was eight, my husband felt sure he wasn't a cat who would live to be old. He had strange spells of ill health, when he spent a lot of time dozing. Then he'd seem better—alert and young again and would bound about like a kitten and, just as we were feeling happier about him, he'd be 'under the weather' again. He had everything we could give him in feeding and veterinary care but we couldn't save him.

One beautiful summer day in 1970, when Bing was ten and a half—no age for a cat—I opened a tin of salmon for a sandwich lunch and turned round to give him the skin and bones. This was his great pleasure and delight and never, never in the years he'd lived with us had I opened a tin of salmon without his being on the spot for what he regarded as his own special privilege. But this time he wasn't there.

I called and called and he didn't come. By three o'clock he still hadn't come and we started to worry. Perhaps he was trapped, or shut in, or hurt. Perhaps some fool with a gun had shot him. When the sun started to go down we were thoroughly upset. He never stayed away, or went very far. Even when we'd moved, he'd shown clearly that he was determined not to get lost. Something must be wrong and soon it would be dark and the foxes would be out. We searched frantically and the dogs searched with us.

In the last of the daylight, Bess, and my husband found him, asleep in the long grass, and brought him back to the house. But he didn't want his salmon, that I'd saved for him, or any of the titbits we offered him during the next few days, and he died very early one morning, with my husband sitting beside him.

All the dogs (perhaps I ought to say 'all the *other* dogs') missed him. He'd shared the hearthrug with them on winter evenings, sprawled out in the sun with them in the summer, gone for walks with them, curled up close to one of them when he didn't feel well. If he stayed out later than the dogs—prowling and hunting as cats will—they worried about him and when he came in they'd lift their heads and he'd run round and give each one of them a quick kiss. They all looked for him in the days after his death and tails and ears drooped to half-mast when they realised he wasn't there. But Tramp had been his special friend and for a long time she sat at the top of the bank, waiting for him to come bounding through the trees as he used to. And finally she got up, and sighed, and we found her whimpering softly outside the old disused pigsty, where we'd dumped Bing's bed and blanket because we didn't like to see them around any longer.

We've never had another cat. We say it's because it wouldn't be fair to the birds, who are now so tame they bang on the kitchen window when they want crumbs, or the fieldmice who pop out of their holes, on the bank behind the house, for the cheese we save for them. But that is only partly true.

Old age—and in Shane's case accident—have claimed all the old gang now and we're down to Sally, who was dumped at the dogs' home just a few hours after she'd produced eight pups. And Sally is very nice—but she is not Rex or Bess or Tramp or Shane and if we had another cat it wouldn't be Bing. So for the time being at least, we'd rather keep our memories.

That's not all he left us. He taught me a whole lot about cats— and dogs too (and I thought I knew a lot about them already).

Although he decided to be one of the dogs, Bing was essentially a cat. He knew all about coming when he was called and could do it as promptly as a dog—but he did it only if it happened to coincide with his own wishes. His favourite trick, when called in for the night, was to stroll pleasantly towards me, let me bend down to pick him up and then he'd shoot off across the lawn or up a tree. He thought this was hilarious and would repeat it up to a dozen times—especially if it happened to be cold and windy outside. I swear he counted on the fact that we were too soft to shut the door and leave him out all night. I wouldn't accept this behaviour from a dog but—after a few furious clashes of wills—I learned to accept it from Bing. I also had to admit—very reluctantly—that we couldn't stop him catching birds and mice. We could stop the dogs killing baby rabbits—we were even able to teach Bess and Shane that it was 'right' to kill a rat and 'wrong' to kill a rabbit— but although I don't doubt Bing was intelligent enough to know what we meant, he didn't agree with our namby-pamby attitude. He was a hunting man to the end. I learned to accept, too, that if he wanted his dinner early, it was better to let him have it. Sticking out for routine was too wearing on the nerves. I'd never, much as I love them, let a dog dictate to me about when he had his dinner. Bing was a cat all right.

But most of all he taught me that you don't have to love dogs *or* cats. Why not both? It worked fine in our family. And if cats and dogs why not other combinations? People have often said to us 'I suppose you don't like children—you think so much of your animals.' But we do like children. We can't see how one excludes the other. And one Christmas when I was collecting toys for some sick children someone rounded on me and said 'Why do you only like children? What about old people? And animals? And refugees? . . .' No wonder the world is in a sad state, when love is so rationed and pigeon-holed.

Every year, for many years now, I've answered hundreds of letters from people who want guidance about pet keeping. And quite a lot of these letters say 'We'd like a cat, only we've got a dog . . .' Or 'The children want a dog, but we've got a cat . . .'

Then there is a lot of advice I can give: introducing a pup and a kitten is easy—usually they make friends right away. Introducing a pup to an adult cat, or a kitten to an adult dog, is not usually too hard—most animals are tolerant of babies, two or four legged. When both cat and dog are adult, there may be some difficulties but they can be overcome with patience. Gain the confidence of the new pet before introducing it; make very sure that the 'old' one is not allowed to feel jealous or resentful or in any way threatened by the newcomer. Be watchful for any aggression, firm if it happens. But let them take their own time about making friends. For the first few weeks—or even months—be satisfied if they tolerate each other. Affection usually comes in time.

Expect them to be friends. Animals pick up our moods very quickly (that's what causes a good deal of dog fighting and cat chasing). If we are tense and apprehensive, they will sense it, and react.

When the 'new' pet is a cat, and you've always had dogs, remember that even the cuddliest kitten has something wild in him. Kipling talked about the cat who 'walked by himself' and no one has ever put it more neatly. Cats often love us but they don't give up their independence as dogs do. They sometimes want to please us but they can't be disciplined or trained. Smack a cat and he'll despise you. Really hurt or frighten him and he'll go off and find himself another home, or live wild. He can, and he will, if you upset him.

But most of all, when I get letters asking whether you can have a cat and a dog, I like to tell people about Bing ('this is what I did' is usually more interesting and more helpful than 'this is what you should do') and how he lived with our gang of dogs and almost believed he was one of them.

And I hope this will help them to decide to become a dog-*and*-cat family and that they will have as much fun watching them, and loving them, as we did.

THE CAT—Though an animal of prey, is a useful domestic. It is neither wanting in sagacity nor sentiment; but its attachments are stronger to places than to persons. The form of its body corresponds with its disposition. The cat is handsome, light, adroit, cleanly, and voluptuous : he loves ease, and searches out the softest furniture in order to respose on, and rest himself.

Cats go with young fifty-five or fifty-six days; they are not so prolific as dogs, and their usual number is four, five or six. Young cats are gay, lively, pretty and would be very proper to amuse children, if the strokes of their paws were not to be feared. Their disposition, which is an enemy to all restraint, renders them incapable of a regular education.

Buffon's Natural History, 1792

Cat's head can be a large green cooking apple or, locally in Ireland, a nodule of gritstone or shale. In different parts of England cat's brain can describe a soil of coarse clay and stones or sandstone traversed by fine streaks of calcite.

GILEAN DOUGLAS, *Cats in our language*

Our wild, hungry Irish cat

THURLOW CRAIG

Several weeks ago two black kittens that had lost their mother came looking for help from us.

Once in the kitchen it only took a few hours for them to be perfectly at home. Gretchen, our big Dobermann bitch, immediately took to mothering them.

These cats are descended from a wild little polydactyl or many-fingered cat who came out of the forest over 15 years ago, adopted us, had a family and then abandoned us, returning to the wild life.

They are all small, with little heads and huge ears but the poly-dactyl strain has dwindled through the years. When a friend who lives in Ireland told us that he knew of a polydactyl black kitten and would we like it, we gratefully accepted.

A few days ago, quite unexpectedly, his car stopped on Top Road in the passing-bay by our gate and out he got, with the promised many-fingered black kitten wrapped in a white terry towel. Carefully closing all doors, we let her go, and with a wild Irish yell she shot under the television table, crouching, lashing her tail, snarling at the resident kittens.

It has always been our custom never to feed a cat about to embark on a long journey, and occasionally, with a highly-bred or nervous animal, it is wise to give a tranquilliser tablet.

In this case Kilkenny Kate (as we immediately named her) had not needed a tranquilliser but after a 12-hour trip by car and steamer was ravenous. Again in such cases it is advisable not to let them eat too much at first; so my wife put down a dish with some warm milk.

Immediately Kate was transformed. Instead of fearful language in a foreign tongue, she burst into loud international purrs, rubbed her head against my wife's hand—nearly spilling the milk—and generally made a fuss of her before daintily lapping up some milk, after which she accepted about a teaspoonful of fishy kitten food.

That done, she washed her face with huge front paws, came out from under the table and jumped up on my knees to make a fuss of me.

Obviously this new acquisition was going to be a great success.

Meanwhile the resident kittens emerged from under the dresser, investigated the remains of the meal and proceeded to ignore Kate in a marked manner, both going into Gretchen's box and lying down against her side, establishing the fact, even if Kate was purring on my knee, they had prior rights to Gretchen.

The curious thing about Kate is, although she cannot possibly be any blood relation to our strain, she is exactly like them. She is slightly older than they, but will always be a small cat with a very neat little head and disproportionately big ears.

Now Gretchen, to the obvious disgust of her adopted children, came out of her box to investigate. Kate, who had never before seen so colossal a dog, shot up onto my shoulder a cursing blue streak, eyes blazing, tail like a flue-brush, back arched and all claws out.

But here again, having made her protest, she examined Gretchen with interest, even allowing Gretchen to lick her.

For the next three days Kate was odd-girl-out to the other kittens, but gradually they relented. Now all is friendliness and they seem to spend most of their waking-hours wrestling, chasing one another all over the place and getting in the way of people's feet.

2
Famous Breeds

Creating a new breed

ANGELA SAYER

Over the centuries the domestic cat has evolved from a small vicious, weasel-like creature of arboreal habits, to the purring, furry animal that graces our hearth-rug today. In the beginning the nearest recognisable ancestors of our pet cats were tabby in marking, for obvious reasons of camouflage. Some were marbled, some striped and some spotted in pattern—depending on their habitat and the climate—some coats were very short and close-lying, others coarse and long with a soft undercoat, capable of bushing out for insulation against the cold. Occasionally the tabby would appear in a deep rufous shade and from time to time a jet-black mutation would occur or, more rarely still, a pure white 'sport'. It is from this limited range of Nature's colours that the many breeds of domestic cat seen today have been developed, some originally by natural selection and many more by the design of man.

Strictly speaking, there are only two breeds of cat, the long-haired and the shorthaired, the latter being sub-divided into two distinct types, one stocky and round of head and eye, the other long and svelte. It is the permutations of these two hair lengths and two distinct types, with the range of coat colours and patterns, that form the formidable list of 'breeds' now seen on the show benches of the cat world.

Since the days of the Crusades, when returning armies carried home unusual cats as presents for their children, a form of selection, albeit unconscious, has been carried out, certain offspring showing unusual or rare coloration being retained and allowed to mature and breed. Towards the end of the nineteenth century, there was quite a vogue for the more exotic cats and in 1871 Harrison Weir, writer, artist and great lover of cats, conceived the idea of holding a cat show at the Crystal Palace, London. This event caused a great stir and was very successful, followed shortly by similar cat shows in the USA and other parts of the world. The exhibition of any type of animal promotes general interest and the showing of cats was no exception. Selections were made and planned matings were arranged. Registration bodies were formed and the first pedigrees written down for posterity. Clubs and societies were formed, some catering for the specialists and others for any cat-lover and carefully formulated standards of points were arrived at and published as a guide to perfection in breeding.

At the turn of the century, the longhaired or Persian cats were the most popular and were very similar to those of the present time. A few Siamese cats were imported from Thailand and were delicate, often being treated like the popular hot-house plants of that era, and domestic shorthaired cats in blue and tabby were greatly admired.

Many of the 'breeds' of today have existed for a number of years and have been fixed in type and conformation by the mating of like-to-like cats for several generations and the subsequent building of written pedigree records. These include, among others, the blue, white, red and tabby longhaired; most of the 'British' varieties; the Siamese in seal, blue and chocolate points and the Abyssinian. Other varieties seen on the show benches today have evolved virtually by accident, when both parents in a planned mating have proved to carry hitherto unknown recessive genes which, when paired up in the resultant offspring, have given rise to a 'new' colour or other characteristic feature. An instance of this occurred in the Siamese, which was originally genetically 'black' and because of the special Siamese factor which restricts the colour to the points of the cat only, appeared as seal-pointed. Simple genetic changes diluted the pigment, causing a brown effect known as chocolate-pointed, or in some cases a blue effect, known as blue-pointed. Mated like-to-like, these three colours in Siamese became known as standard 'natural' varieties. When two Siamese were mated together, each carrying both blue and chocolate genes, however, very pale ethereal-looking kittens began to appear, and it was thought at first that these were bad blue-points. Eventually, with more genetic knowledge of cats becoming available, it was realised that this was in fact a new colour variety, the lilac-pointed Siamese, and mated together, two lilac-points would only produce lilac-pointed kittens.

Other naturally evolved breeds include the red Abyssinian, the first kittens arriving quite without precedent in otherwise normally coloured litters of pure-bred Abyssinian parentage. Spontaneous mutations account for the Manx cats, whose taillessness, and habit of bunny-hopping is well known and also, more recently, for the appearance of the Rex cats. The first Rex to be born was noticed in a litter of kittens born to a quite ordinary-looking tortoiseshell queen on a farm in Cornwall in 1950. It was not known which of the local toms had sired the little male kitten, with its most unusual tightly curled coat and whiskers, but the owner was intrigued by his crinkled appearance and sought advice, eventually mating him back to his mother, thus producing a litter with more curly kittens and the start of a very popular variety—the Cornish Rex. About ten years later, a similar kitten was noticed in a litter born in Devon and it was at once thought that these curled cats were somehow related. However intermating between this cat and the Cornish Rex proved disappointing, with only straight-coated kittens being born, proving that a completely different gene was involved and this kitten was the founder of the Devon Rex strain. Both types of Rex cat proved very popular and were allowed in any normally acceptable coat colour or pattern and the standards laid down for their breeding are similar, calling for long, slender bodies, limbs and tails. The heads are quite different however, the Cornish being very oriental and straight in profile, while the Devon must have a pronounced 'stop' in the nose.

Despite the great range and variety of naturally evolved cats, fanciers throughout the world have constantly striven for new types and more and more are developed each decade. Given the natural colour range, the naturally occurring dilutions such as cream and blue, the two body types, the two hair lengths, and then the occasional mutation also, it can be seen that the permutations in cat breeding are virtually endless. The art of experimental or progressive breeding lies in the ability to bring to the surface, as it were, the desired characteristics of the dream cat, each person having his or her own idea of the make-up of this dream creature. Few combinations of traits are impossible to achieve, although it is unlikely that the size of the domestic cat can ever be changed to a great extent. It seems impossible to produce cats larger than fifteen pounds or so, although cats which revert to the wild occasionally grow much larger in the feral state. Attempts at miniaturisation have failed, owing to sterility in the F_1 progeny.

Many now established breeds have evolved almost by accident. The tabby-pointed Siamese is an excellent example. The first tabby-pointed kittens were exhibited at a London cat show and caused quite a stir. Their mother, also a tabby-point, was the result of a Siamese seal-point having a *mésalliance* with a tabby male, obviously with Siamese ancestry. The interest shown in these kittens was sufficient for other, planned, breeding programmes to be commenced, and the tabby-point Siamese is now well established in the world of show cats.

Many of the older and well-established breeders in the Cat Fancy have little knowledge of genetics and concentrate exclusively on their own favourite breed. They abhor any attempts to standardise a new variety, and often openly condemn attempts by more progressive fanciers to create a new colour variety or type in the cat. Their main fear seems to be that, if a cat of their own breed is used in the initial matings in an experimental breeding programme, this old-established breed will become contaminated in some way and spoiled for ever.

Those more scientifically inclined can see quite clearly that this cannot possibly happen unless hybrid kittens fall into the hands of unscrupulous people, for the initial crosses are but the very first step in the production of a new variety and are used only to introduce differences in coat or eye colour, hair length and so on. Experimental breeding, as it is often and incorrectly called, is an expensive and time-consuming practice and is never undertaken lightly. Those who do decide to develop a new breed are dedicated cat fanciers with space, time and sufficient income to maintain a number of cats in proper conditions and with no like-lihood of recouping the outlay. Anyone who attempts to embark upon a planned breeding programme to produce a new variety, without these prerequisites, will fail miserably.

To produce a new breed, it is essential to ascertain whether or not it will be attractive to the general public and be demanded as a pet, for it is pointless to produce an end product that no one wants! Then it must be decided whether it is a genetic possibility, for it is equally pointless to strive after some characteristic for year after year if it is unlikely to be achieved in the end. It must next be decided whether or not the cat is to be longhaired or shorthaired, of foreign or British type, what coat pattern and colour is desired and which of the genetic factors involved are dominant or recessive to which other factors. Having established a clear idea of the finished variety, a rough standard of points should be drawn up and a careful breeding plan formulated.

The basic stock selected for the breeding of a new variety must be very carefully chosen. They should have good breeding records and must be healthy and sound without any skeletal defects. Breeding tests must be carried out to determine any genetic factors they might carry which would prove a setback to the breeding programme or add undesirable characteristics to the new variety. It is generally accepted by progressive breeders in Great Britain that they will have to eventually prove three clear generations of like-to-like matings of their new variety in order to stand any chance of gaining recognition of that variety by the British regis-tration body, the Governing Council of the Cat Fancy.

Three generations of such breeding may or may not 'fix' the desired traits in the new cat but most conscientious breeders agree to the rule and work to this end. Progressive breeding is not to be undertaken lightly, or by the novice, as a considerable genetic knowledge is necessary for satisfactory progress to be made. Many kittens are produced during the formation of a new breed which fall short of the standards required and these kittens have to be run on and neutered before going to new pet homes. Some of these 'half-way' kittens are strikingly attractive and occasionally a hybrid kitten is found to be so appealing in its own right that yet another new variety is conceived from that offshoot.

One such example of a new variety stemming from a breeding programme for an entirely different end product is that of the Egyptian Mau. During the first generations of the breeding for tabby-pointed Siamese, a striking half-Siamese foreign tabby was mated to a top-class, seal-pointed Siamese and in the resultant litter there were several tabby-pointed Siamese and one foreign tabby, classed as a 'reject' by the breeder. This tabby kitten had superior type however, better than her acceptable brothers and sisters and a striking resemblance was noticed between her and the cats depicted upon the Egyptian scrolls. From this little 'reject' kitten has evolved the present strain of bronze Egyptian Mau cats, now being bred in the third generation, which faithfully reproduce in colour and markings the sacred cat of the Ancient Egyptians, complete with distinctive scarab marking between the ears.

Another fairly recent addition to the Siamese ranks is the red-pointed Siamese. A first cross was necessary to introduce the red colour into the Siamese and problems occur with any cross involving the natural red or ginger, as this is sex-linked as will be seen below. A red female cat was mated to a very good seal-point Siamese and the resultant litter contained red males and tortoiseshell females. Each carried the Siamese factor, which is recessive to self-colour, and had the green eye colour of the mother, not the sapphire blue of the sire. Mated together with her red brother, a tortoiseshell female produced a seal-point male and a red-point male plus a little female like herself—tortoiseshell all over. The possibility of offspring in her litter was for males to be seal-point and red-point Siamese, self-black and self-red and the females to be tortoiseshell or tortoiseshell-pointed Siamese. To produce a red pointed Siamese female, one of the tortoiseshell-pointed offspring had to be mated to a red-pointed male. Unfortunately the early attempts at breeding red-points were not greeted favourably by the Cat Fancy in general as the original kittens were of such poor foreign type. Early breeders of the variety mated litter mates together *inter se* in order to achieve the desired colour effect without concentrating too much on type. It would have been more beneficial to the red-pointed Siamese, as a breed variety, had a longer breeding programme been undertaken at the outset, mating back to top-class, seal-point stock and producing high-quality, interim tortie-points before attempting to breed the red-point females. However new programmes were started eventually and cats of acceptable type were bred, resulting in the granting of a breed number and championship status in 1965.

In longhaired cats the most recent man-made varieties have been the colour-point or Himalayan. These are Persian in type and

'Who said we weren't friends?'
A cat is not a dog . . . or is he?

A demure Self Chocolate kitten—one of the newest of breeds

The latest in the States but descended from the original Angoras—
Turkish Angora kittens

conformation but with Siamese colouring—the Himalayan coat
pattern, as this is termed by geneticists. Originally bred in the
four basic Siamese colours of seal, blue, chocolate and lilac, the
red and tortie-point colour-points also have full championship
status. Basically the colour-point Persian was bred by mating a
longhaired black female with a Siamese male. Because longhair is
recessive to shorthair and Siamese is recessive to full colour, the
kittens were all shorthaired blacks *but*, each carried the genes for
longhair and Siamese colouring. Matings between this first generation gave longhaired blacks, shorthaired blacks, shorthaired
Siamese-patterned and longhaired Siamese-patterned. The type
of these kittens was intermediate, neither as 'Persian' as a longhaired cat should be, nor as 'Foreign' as a Siamese. The eye colour
of the Siamese-patterned kittens was blue but not of the intensity
of a pure Siamese. Much work was needed to develop the Himalayan cats, as seen on the show benches today, from these first
specimens and the few dedicated breeders who have achieved
these results are to be congratulated. Offshoots from the colour-
point breeding programmes have resulted in two more delightful
varieties, the self-chocolate longhaired and the self-lilac longhaired, still very much in their infancy.

It should not be long before we see tabby-pointed colour-
points at our shows and surely a chocolate tabby-pointed longhair
would be a most attractive exhibit?

The most recent additions to the show ranks in the Foreign
shorthaired section are the Foreign whites and the Foreign
lavenders. Foreign whites are in fact Siamese cats wearing white
overcoats. They are genetically Siamese, with a dominant white
factor, and have the true Siamese-blue eye colour which ensures
that, unlike some other blue-eyed white cats, they are never deaf.
It was on receipt of an over-exposed photograph of some Siamese
kittens, making them look white all-over instead of with coloured
points, that made one of the three original breeders of this variety
conceive the idea of self-white Foreign cats. Matings between
white cats and top-class Siamese for six or seven generations have
been carried out to date and like-to-like matings to conform with
the regulations of the Governing Council have been commenced,
so it is likely that this charming sparkling white variety will soon
have the championship status it deserves.

Creating the Foreign lavender is an exercise in how to produce
a new variety. Genetically a 'self' lilac-point Siamese, the standards

D

decided upon were for extreme Siamese type and conformation, oriental eyes of a vivid apple-green and a short coat of a faded lavender shade. Tabby markings and yellow eye colour was made taboo and the kink, allowable in Siamese, was deplored. Another undesirable trait found in many contemporary Siamese, the weak chin, was also to be treated as undesirable and the foundation stock was carefully chosen so that several unrelated lines could be bred simultaneously. For one line, which has proved most successful, a pair of Havana cats (genetically Havana is self-chocolate Siamese), each with a lilac-pointed sire and a Havana dam, were mated together. As expected the litter consisted of Havana, self-lavender, chocolate-point and lilac-point Siamese. These first generation lavender kittens were mated on maturity to other first generation lavender kittens from a different line and thus the variety was started. The type in these first kittens was outstandingly good, because of the careful selection in the basic stock, so it was permissible to carry out like-to-like matings straight away. Had the type been poor, back-crossing to lilac-point Siamese of outstanding type would have been necessary to 'fix' this conformation in the new variety. However, in these particular lines, type has been consistently good and kittens have been produced which are free from the Siamese restriction factor and may thus be deemed 'pure' Foreign lavender.

Many new varieties are still feasible. We could quite simply achieve British browns and lilacs, Siamese–Manx, apricot smoke Foreign shorthairs and many, many others and it is reasonable to assume that while cat breeding continues to be so popular, progressive breeders will continue to explore the possible permutations provided by Nature, producing many more beautiful breeds of the domestic cat.

The Turkish angora: revival of an ancient breed

ALETHA HENDRICKSON

American cat fanciers are enjoying the reincarnation of a breed once thought to be extinct: the Turkish angora. The angora had not been registered or shown since 1899 owing to interbreeding with Persians and other breeds but, as a result of recent imports from Turkey, the angora has made a strong comeback on the United States and Canadian show scene.

Angoras were well known in the US and in England prior to the 1880s. Various writers of the nineteenth century described the breed as having attributes seen in today's Turkish angora. Its ruff was known as 'the Queen Elizabeth ruffle'. The long tail, with its full brush, was described as being supple and expressive. Colours were well known and accepted: the solid and mixed colours such as smoke, various tabbies, creams (buffs), blacks, blues and others, as well as all eye colours of whites.

Most authorities recognise that the angora is a pure natural breed of cat originating in the area of Ankara, Turkey. Two centuries ago, angoras were brought to the Americas by sea traders and later were brought over from England, France and other European countries. The cats were so well thought of that a New York fancier is reported to have imported a male angora from France, valued at $5,000!

Unfortunately for the breed, the angoras were used indiscriminately in Persian breeding programmes. For a time, 'Persian' and 'angora' names were used interchangeably to denote the Persian–angora cross. In time, the Persian qualities dominated and the angora disappeared from the show scene. However, the public still generally thought of any long-nosed, longhaired breed of cat as 'angora' and still do so today.

The older writings concerning angoras described a lovely long-haired breed in detail. Comparisons of older descriptions with those of today show that the breed is much as it was in former times. The head is wedge-shaped—but not extremely so. A strong chin and jaw are desirable. The ears are set high on the head and are long, pointed, and sport exotic tufts from inside the ears, which sometimes reach to the lower portion of the cheek.

The almond-shaped eyes give unique expression to this exquisite breed. Eye colour can be a sky blue, or sunny clear amber, or one can have the best of two worlds—one amber eye and one blue eye as in the odd-eyed Turkish angora! The eyes are very expressive, sometimes giving a puckish look, or at other moments imparting a regal bearing well suited to a breed of such ancient, Turkish lineage. In repose, or posing in the show ring, the Turkish angora looks as elegant as is possible for any cat to look.

The body-coat colour has already been mentioned but the unique quality of the coat lies really in its texture. It can be likened to the incredible softness of the fur on a rabbit's tummy! With all this beauty and luxuriousness, the breed's coat comes with an added plus—very little grooming is involved as the coat doesn't mat nearly as much as the Persian's. As with all cats, some grooming must however be done but with the Turkish angora this need not be of the same duration or frequency as is the case with other longhaired breeds. The hair on the Turkish angora's stomach is extra fine and wavy, having a silk-like sheen.

The overall appearance of the Turkish angora suggests a medium-sized cat, lithe, agile, light framed and possessing strength and vigour. Yet it also denotes a lovely elegant creature, proudly bearing centuries of beautiful cats in its ancestry.

As early as 1954 an odd-eyed white Turkish angora was imported by a lover of the breed, through the efforts of a serviceman stationed in Turkey. Later, the fancier's interest in the breed heightened and she was able to obtain several other white Turkish angoras from the Istanbul Zoo through the services of a native of Turkey, resident in the United States. A line of these cats was established and as they produced not only whites, but bi-colours and other colours, the Canadian Cat Association accepted them eventually for registration. The stock is registered in the other associations in America including the Cat Fanciers' Association (CFA).

In 1962 a native Turkish importer, now too living in America, obtained an odd-eyed white female from private Turkish breeders from the city of Ankara, who had established a Turkish angora breeding programme. In 1968 he imported five other Turkish angoras from the same source. Although his participation in working with the breed was short-lived, his stock is now well established, having been dispersed throughout the United States and Canada. They are registered with all associations including the CFA. It must be noted here that some of his stock was bred with Persian and Siamese, resulting in hybrids accepted by only three of the American registering associations as being Turkish angoras. Naturally they are not and the CFA and the other associations will accept only those Turkish angoras whose ancestry can be traced directly to Turkey.

The two importers so far mentioned worked with cats considered somewhat controversial by some in both the US and Turkey. Although the coloured angoras were obviously accepted centuries ago, some fanciers insist that only white angoras are authentic. The Turkish people themselves are divided in their opinion of what constitutes the true angora—some say that only the deaf, odd-eyed white is the true one and others insist that the angora comes in many colours as well as white. The white theorists point to a legend that the Turkish people's beloved Attaturk will return some day in the guise of an odd-eyed deaf Turkish angora. But US fanciers generally refute the 'white-only' theory because it is well known that the whites from 'white-only' catteries have produced coloured Turkish angoras! In fact, Turkish angoras from all sources in Turkey, including the Istanbul Zoo, the city of Ankara and the Ankara Zoo, have produced colours.

The American associations started accepting the Turkish angora for registration and championships at the end of the 1960s. The CFA, CCA and CFF accepted them for championship competition in 1973, while the ACFA, ACA, ICF, and NCFA accepted them for championship status in 1972. All associations register whites and colours, though most of them accept only whites at this time for championships. ICF accepts the colours for championship competition and the CFA accepts them for AOV showing. It would seem colours are definitely here to stay and certain colours in Turkish angoras are very much in demand by American exhibitors and breeders.

In 1962 an American colonel and his wife imported a pair of white Turkish angoras from the Ankara Zoo. A year later they imported another white pair from the same source. These cats are registered with the CFA and all other associations and the lines are also widely being used by various breeders.

In 1964 another service-connected importer returned to the United States with a white pair from the Ankara Zoo. Two other importers also imported a white male and a white female from the Ankara Zoo. These cats were all duly registered with the CFA and their lines are being used throughout the country, the offspring having been registered with all associations.

Two organisations were formed to further the interests of the Turkish angora. The first, The Turkish Angora Society, founded late on in 1971, later became The Original Turkish Angora Society. It is not affiliated to any cat association, has a monthly newsletter and maintains that white Ankara Zoo cats are the only authentic Turkish angoras. The author founded the other organisation in December 1971 and it was affiliated to the CFA in January 1972. The organisation was first known as The Turkish Angora Club of the East, later changing its name to the National Turkish Angora Cat Club, to reflect its national membership. The NTACC now has more than 40 members in 14 states and Canada and publishes a bi-monthly newsletter which is sent to subscribers, cat magazines and all CFA board members and judges.

Through the efforts of its members, the Turkish angora was accepted for championship in CFA starting with the 1973–4 show season. The club numbers among its members: CFA board members, CFA judges, leaders of Pet Pride, Inc. and breeders, exhibitors and owners of Turkish angoras. The red fez is the NTACC's symbol and members can be readily recognised at cat shows by the red fez jauntily perched upon a slender dowel atop the cages containing the Turkish angoras entered!

The NTACC maintains several kinds of services for its members. A stud registrar keeps a file of all available proven registered Turkish angora studs for inquiries requesting stud service. It also employs the services of a kitten registrar who maintains a file of CFA-registered Turkish angora kittens to service inquiries for kittens. Probably the most helpful of services to Turkish angora owners and breeders is the NTACC stud book, which contains the pedigrees of authentic Turkish angoras so that anyone might trace an authentic Turkish angora back to Turkey. The stud book also contains the pedigrees of so-called angoras who have been bred to other breeds, so that those wishing to maintain purity of the breed may know which lines to avoid.

While earlier writings speak of the Turkish angora's appearance and colours, little if anything is mentioned of its habits and endearing personality. The Turkish angora is absolutely immaculate in its personal habits. Even the studs are as fastidious in their toilet habits as their sisters. They readily adapt to most kinds of good litter and it is essential that their boxes be frequently changed as they require clean litter. They delight in standing on the rims of their boxes. Wise owners put a brick or two against them to keep the boxes against the wall, thereby eliminating tip-over problems. Turkish angoras also take great pleasure in scratching certain types of litter out of their boxes. We know of one male in particular who prefers water for his elimination procedures. Since the owner did not know him well enough to provide a water pan for him instead of a litter pan, he used his water dish for his litter box exclusively and he slept in the clean litter in his litter pan! The owner quickly adjusted to his unusual habits and provided an off-the-floor drinking arrangement for him so that he could have his fresh water and still have his *water* litter pan.

The breed's cleanliness manifests itself not only in litter habits but also in personal bathing. A very few Turkish angoras rather enjoy a soap and water bath but the vast majority prefer to clean themselves. Naturally the well-groomed Turkish angora should be bathed prior to a show—but between times, and for the average angora as a pet, their own 'bathing schedule' should suffice most of the time. After each meal, it becomes time for the Turkish angora to tend to his washing ritual. Much attention is paid to the face, ears, whiskers and paws. Extra effort is spent on the tail and tummy area. If a cat runs out of body of his own to clean, he will start in on a companion he feels needs additional washing!

Some of the more fastidious Turkish angoras will spend much time after meals trying to scratch (an invisible) covering over their meal dish. If they are fed on a place mat or cloth, this can result in the food bowl being camouflaged under a heap of cloth. Some cats spend much time at this, thinking that only the very astute will discover the whereabouts of their feed dish.

Turkish angoras readily adapt to most kinds of varied quality diets. They have good appetites and don't tend to fat because they are active. They need and deserve a good diet designed for their specific nutritional needs. They should have cooked and raw beef and lamb organs, deboned poultry, cooked deboned fish and cottage cheese. Additional supplements might include vitamins, oil, debitterised yeast tablets fed from the hand, strained baby meats for trips and shows and non-fat milk powder. Some Turkish angora's tastes tend to more exotic fare such as potato chips and spaghetti but such forbidden treats should be given only very occasionally. One cat of our breeding is particularly enamoured of Chinese food!

We find the Turkish angora a very robust and hardy breed—given the proper diet and fresh air, exercise, care and love. Only the most filthy and inhumane conditions will finally get to the breed's rugged constitution. The ordinary precautions against feline distemper, fleas, ticks, ear mites and worms should be employed of course.

Recently we had an unusually rough winter storm in Maryland and we were without heat, electricity, water and fuel of any kind for three days. Rescue workers were busy with the elderly and infants, so we had to fend for ourselves. Our children were sent to a neighbouring farm which at least had a fireplace but my husband and I decided not to leave our cats, dogs and farm animals. The *inside* temperature of our home dropped to 26°— the water in the cats' dishes froze solid.

We realised the immediate need for water and, since a farmer had generously brought over an old Coleman kerosene stove and fuel, we melted snow to make water for the animals and ourselves. We had eight cats, two of them, four-month-old kittens, a Persian (now a CFA Grand Champion) and a Turkish angora. We put them both in an airline crate, covered it with newspapers and covered the whole thing with blankets. The studs proved to be a particular problem; we put them in a bathroom with a HHP neuter. Taking a wire dog-crate, we lit ten candles, taking care that they were well in the crate so that the cats couldn't get to the fire. The heat from the candles and the energy expended as the cats hissed, spat and generally carried on with each other proved their salvation!

The remaining females were put two to a shipping crate (for cosiness) and placed around the Coleman stove. We covered the crates with blankets except for the side facing the stove. Then we got into bed ourselves with as many blankets as we could find and 'thought warm'. All this is to relate the hardiness of the breed. Not one cat, or kitten, suffered so much as a sniffle. They all survived beautifully, even if there were some hard feelings among the studs and neuter over territorial rights in the bathroom. (Incidentally, we learned our lesson and obtained two Coleman stoves, a supply of kerosene and built a fireplace so that we and our pets wouldn't be caught in that predicament again!) While the breed can survive cold temperatures, it can stand hot ones too as is evidenced by their remaining comfortable in our hot (90°–100°) summers.

The temperament of the Turkish angora has individual variations but apparent in all is innate intelligence and natural affection. Naturally some ill-bred (inbred for far too many generations) and poorly raised (in cramped environments with insufficient human attention and love) specimens are hard to handle at times. But the vast majority of Turkish angoras are affectionate loving creatures and are easily handled both at home and in the show ring.

They have a selection of 'words' that owners learn to interpret. Cat-owners all know the insistent 'Meeoooowwww!' heard at meal times. Turkish angoras also emit charming 'Brrrrrrrrp' and 'Chirrrrrrrip' sounds when they are especially happy. Some have an inquiring 'Brrp?' when a new toy or new kitten is introduced. When about to go on a playful spree, they announce their willingness to play with a short series of 'Chrrps!'

Purring is one of the most endearing aspects of any cat and the Turkish angora exhibits a loving personality. Purring is heard anytime the cat is satisfied. One of our cats starts purring the moment she is touched or we enter a room. At times the purring is accompanied by kneading. One female we have is quite a professional kneader, almost rivalling a high-stepping majorette as she raises her front feet high off the floor.

Favourite toys include: crumpled-up paper, empty thread spools, open paper bags, cardboard boxes, ping-pong balls, coiled pipe cleaners and just about anything that isn't nailed down. Some intelligent Turkish angoras even retrieve—we have one who does so consistently. When she tires of 'throw and fetch', she takes off with the object. We never see it again and we suspect she has quite a cache hidden somewhere.

Although deafness in cats carrying the blue-eyed white gene is considered by some to be a problem, it can be an added asset. One Turkish angora actually rides a vacuum cleaner around the room as her owner cleans. The other cats scramble away because of the racket but this deaf cat isn't afraid because she can't hear the noise. For the same cat, her owner's bath and shower is an exciting playtime. She is unaware of the noise of the splashing and considers the whole thing much fun. Her owner communicates with her by hand signals, tapping and vibrations. Extreme awareness and intelligence enables this cat to interpret her owner's meanings and some undiscovered force tells her when the refrigerator door opens for meal times. This cat is also extra calm at shows—the attendant noise doesn't disturb her unduly.

The good nature and high spirits of the breed stay with them throughout adulthood. Although they are most active as kittens and young adults, they romp and play even as grown cats. Stairs are favourite sites for running, doors are made for sitting atop, or hiding behind for the less athletic specimens, and windows are dandy to keep track of wildlife.

We have a Persian and Turkish angora who spend every morning at the window overlooking our garden making certain the birds are all well. We suspect if the cats were allowed a closer inspection of the birds, that all would *not* be well with the birds' health! But these two dedicated bird-watchers spend about an hour each morning observing their feathered friends. We have many good reasons for maintaining that all cats are better kept in the home or on screened porches rather than being allowed to run loose. One of the most important of these reasons is the damage a Turkish angora would inflict on our diminishing wildlife if he were allowed access to it.

As do most pets, a Turkish angora likes to be comfortable.

Their favourite sleeping place is in the middle of their owner's bed. But other places suffice too and our cats enjoy themselves on shelves, windows (securely screened so as to prevent falls), tops of buffets and the refrigerator. One cat has a favourite chair which happens to be the one at my place at the kitchen table. If I sit in it, she gets off but she soon returns, wedging herself between me and the back of the chair, surreptitiously forcing me out until she has regained sole possession of it once again. She is so attached to this chair that when the kitchen is scrubbed and the chair is lifted out of the way onto a table, she remains in the chair while it is being moved and lifted.

Although the Turkish angora is making a great comeback in the American show rings, its greatest achievement is the position it occupies in the hearts of those privileged to own one. The Turkish angora is an ancient breed, of exquisite beauty and fascinating ways. To know and own one is to love one!

Cat's eye is a gem, which cut *en cabochen* (carbuncle-shaped), shows a line of light across the dome. (In oriental countries it is the chrysoberyl and in western lands the quartz variety.) But in Australia cat's eye is something else entirely: the operculum of a marine mollusk. In medicine, cat's eye is an eye where the retina has an opalescent look due to the tumor disease, glioma. On the other hand the cat eye is a large, spiny, brilliant-red fish of the North Atlantic which can be found in deep water from New York to Cape Hatteras.

GILEAN DOUGLAS, *Cats in our language*

The Rex

PHYLLIS LAUDER

The Rex cat is the latest arrival on the Cat Fancy scene. A cat with 'broken', wavy fur and crinkled eyebrows and whiskers, first brought to the attention of breeders in 1953. The Korat cat has been known, though not at once recognised, by all the governing bodies for a very long time and if you except the beautiful new Burmese colours and the many and varied new points colours in Siamese, there is no more recent addition to the list of fancy cats than the Rex.

It was a lady in Cornwall, Mrs Ennismore, who realised during the 1950s that she had, in a cat named Kallibunker, an unusual mutation of the coat. This cat and his progeny were brought to the attention of Dr A. G. Searle and Mr A. C. Jude and, through them, to the late B. A. Stirling-Webb, an experimental breeder of distinction; he had established the lovely Colourpoints, known in America as Himalayans and, with a group of his friends, he took up the newly discovered Rex cats. Two kittens were exhibited at one of the shows given by the Kensington Kitten Club in London, so that the Fancy might see them. Their waved coats were so unusual as to excite a good deal of comment and they continued to be bred by the group of breeders especially interested in them.

This type of feline fur must have been present in the cat for a very long time, although, as Dr Searle points out, it was never widely established in cat populations until the Fancy came along and took a hand. A curious thing is that the mutation concerned came to the notice of breeders in different parts of the world at approximately the same time. It is not surprising that a lady in Devon, doubtless aware of Mr Stirling-Webb's interest, brought to him a cat, named Kirlee, with wavy fur, from Devonshire. Oddly, however, it so happened that at about the time when Dr Searle first saw Kallibunker, Dr Scheuer-Karpin of Germany found a Rex-coated female in Berlin-Buch: she called this cat Lämmchen —little lamb—and a short time later there appeared in the *Journal of Genetics* a paper by Searle and Jude describing both Cornish and German Rex. To the USA, also, these cats were indigenous: many have been imported from Britain but two strains at least were already present. Oregon Rex, bred by Mrs Mildred Stringham, are American Rex; and in California were discovered some Rex cats with long fur. Abandoned because they were 'funny-looking', they had been rescued and brought to the shelter. They were taken over by two American breeders and the little mother was named Mystery Lady of Rodell.

These cats were referred to as Marcels, because of the difference between them and Rex. They are beautiful as kittens, covered in ringlets but, once they are grown-up, the curls become untidy and the coats difficult to groom, so the strain was not persisted with. Some of the cats, however, crossed with Cornish, are known as Cornish/California Rex. It is to be presumed that, since shorthair in the cat is dominant to longhair, the Marcel coat would eventually tend to disappear. Meantime there have been found, both in Britain and in America, cat populations comprising Rex individuals. Indeed, this mutation was noted in the USA a good many years ago, when it was referred to as Karakul.

There are nearly always set-backs at the inception of anything new and the early Rex breeders found two: a Devon × Cornish cross produced only normal, shorthair kittens; the Cornish cats

with which they had started did not, when mated with the Devon
male discovered later, breed true. Next, it was found that the
Devon Rex cats often had bare patches in their coats. The early
breeders were extremely disappointed when they discovered that
Cornish and Devon were incompatible: they had been delighted
to find an unrelated male and it must have dashed their hopes
when his kittens to their Cornish queens proved to be normal-
coated shorthairs. Both these troubles, however, were to a great
extent overcome. The normal-coated kittens from the Devon and
Cornish cross would, when mated *inter se*, or back to a cat pure
for either variety, have litters which comprised a given proportion
of Rex kittens. And, besides, it was possible for breeders to keep
to one variety only. For instance, there are at present two Cornish
lines in which there is no Devon whatever. As to the bareness, a
great deal has been done to eliminate this, partly by the introduction of longhair into the Devon strain. Very beautiful Devon Rex,
in whom there is no bareness at all, have appeared in the show
pen.

Cornish Rex and German Rex are compatible—mated together
they will have only wavy-coated kittens. This is known because
of the valuable work done by American breeders: Mrs Mable
Tracy and other USA breeders have proved the compatibility of
Cornish and German Rex through test matings carried out in four
lines.

The appearance of the cats is unusual, chiefly because of their
fur: a good Rex coat is thick and deeply waved all over. I handled
a kitten at the National Cat Club's show at the end of 1971 whose
waves extended to his paws, so that he appeared to be wearing
ridged mittens. And indeed the new-born kittens always look as
though they were dressed in little ripple suits! The owner of the
German Rex, Lämmchen, describes the waves as forming whorls
at the end of her tail and beside her ears. The wavy coats are, in
fact, the distinguishing feature of Rex: as Mr Stirling-Webb said
'Without the wavy coats, they would just be ordinary cats.' So
important to this breed is the quality of the fur that in the standard
of points 50 marks are allotted for coat in Cornish Rex and 40
marks for coat in Devon Rex. The reason for this last is that
breeders of Devon Rex cats considered head type of such importance that they wanted extra marks for this feature.

The heads of the Devons are, indeed, so unusual that it is true
to say that they are different from any other feline head. They

have short muzzles, round cheeks and large ears, set low, giving them a pixie-like appearance that is extremely appealing and unusual.

Standards were, of course, discussed and drawn up by committees of interested breeders and more than one provisional standard was accepted *pro tempore*. Today the Rex cats have been bred for a good many generations and so have obtained recognition and championship status.

The first provisional standard gave 'Any colour, as in Manx' and this is still the directive in most of the American standards. In Britain, however, a Cornish Rex with a solid colour and white coat pattern must conform, if he wishes to win at a show, with the official standard for bi-colours in this respect. He will be penalised if he has irregular white markings—perhaps one 'solid' paw, or white hairs here and there in his blue, orange or black coat. A Devon may have no white markings at all. Recently some very beautiful colours have appeared : Rex breeders have produced cats with lilac coats and with fur of a lovely bronze-brown, as well as the already present white coats which, in Devons, stemmed, many of them, from Briarry Waitrose, the Devon Rex with the perfect, deeply waved, thick all-over coat, bred by B. A. Stirling-Webb from longhair ancestry.

The standards make very clear the difference in headshape between Cornish, with medium wedge and Devon, short-faced with decided nose-stop, and it is noteworthy that an important governing body, the American Cat Fanciers' Association, is currently drawing up a separate standard for Devons. Kallibunker, the original English Rex, had long legs with the hind legs slightly higher than the forelegs but his tail, though long, was not 'whippy' and his head, though not as round as those of domestic shorthairs, was not a long one. His type could thus fairly be described as 'modified foreign' and those of his descendants who conform best to the Governing Council standard are the ones whose type is not exaggerated.

The curled *vibrissae* are a most attractive feature of these cats : eyebrows and whiskers are bent and curled and the effect is charming, as is that of the waved coats, which are the distinctive feature. Rex cats have no guard hairs—those silky, straight, long hairs which are present in all other breeds. Their fur consists of down hairs—in the undercoat only, though a few awn hairs, individually thicker than the down hairs, are present in the Devons.

And the down coat may grow so thickly that it is difficult to find the skin.

The Devons have, as their standard indicates, been crossed with Siamese, and some very beautiful Si-Rex have appeared at shows. Whereas the introduction of too much Siamese might tend to spoil the very attractive head shape of this variety, yet this outcross, carefully carried out, has been a good one, bringing greatly improved coats to the breed and producing some lovely cats.

In a list of faults included in the standard is an excellent directive: narrow, long or British-type head would be undesirable. An attractive feature of the ACA standards in the USA consists of very good line drawings of the cats, the one for Rex being particularly good.

In comparison with other breeds, these cats moult very little, though there may be a heavy moult between kittenhood and adulthood and a Rex with a very thick coat needs plenty of brushing and combing. In general, however, only a little fluff will come out in the comb. There is for Rex owners, the great advantage that their furniture will not be covered with moulted fur.

It is not difficult to prepare a Rex cat for a show. The coat should be given an extra combing for a week or more every day before the show, with attention to the possibility of little fleas—for even a short coat may harbour them—and also for the possibility of ear mites. There are good, safe insecticide powders on sale. They can be bought from chemists, and will do no harm to the cat if he licks his fur; but when the ears are concerned, if trouble is present, it is best to consult a vet. If ear mites are there, he will prescribe drops that will quickly clear them away and it is best to be sure that there is nothing more seriously wrong. If the insides of a cat's ears look dirty, treatment should be sought at once for, if the condition is left, the cat will scratch himself violently, to the extent of drawing blood. A sure danger signal is the head-shaking which takes place when the ears are affected.

In the matter of show preparation for Rex it is, as for other cats, advisable to go over the coats gently and firmly with a genuine chamois leather. In a healthy cat this will make the coat ripple and shine and it should be done on several successive days before the show. One breeder goes over the curled whiskers with almond oil as part of show preparation and it is also a good idea, when the great day comes, to give the little contestant only a small breakfast and then, when he is established in his pen, to offer some little

'Who called me a poodle cat?' Cornish Rex

tit-bit that he particularly likes, so that he will feel the show hall is not such a bad place after all.

There is no difficulty in feeding a Rex cat: raw beef, raw ox heart, raw liver—all are good for him and although, like other cats, Rex have their individual preferences, most like steamed white fish. Some are not in the least interested in chicken, turkey or other game birds: these are, perhaps, inclined to be dry. Rabbit is sometimes a treat, though now and then a cat will not care for it. Of two Rex cats I know living together, one would not touch jugged hare while the other loved it. Individual likes and dislikes extend to the matter of drinking also: some drink only water, some like milk, most are pleased with milk laced with blood from raw meat. Rabbit broth is usually acceptable, provided it comes from a rabbit which has been thoroughly cleaned before boiling and provided the liver is removed and not cooked with the rest. Appetites vary; some Rex cats are not greedy and will leave a little food in their dishes, even if it be something they favour, when they have had enough. Naturally a queen in kitten will be insatiably hungry, as she will when she is feeding her kittens. And a litter of growing, healthy kittens can eat a great deal!

Rex are a healthy breed for they have only recently come to the Fancy from mixed populations of domestic cats and have the stamina of their good, strong ancestry. This is not to say that they cannot be ill—it is important to ensure that kittens all have their 'jabs' and essential to seek the vet.-surgeon's help early if there are signs of illness. Only he is really qualified to give advice and little bits of information from books or from friends cannot compare with the opinion of a vet.-surgeon you trust. Usually, however, this is a healthy breed and many of the cats' troubles are accidentally caused: there have been Rex cats who have burned their paw pads on a hot stove, been injured in a fight, even become entangled in barbed wire. They are good patients, fortunately and, since they are constitutionally strong, they usually make good recoveries. Rex queens normally kitten easily and rear their litters successfully: a brood queen in ecstasies over a basketful of new arrivals, all with 'ridged' coats, as if they were wearing little purl-plain knitted suits, is delightful to see—and to hear, for she will purr joyfully to her kittens.

These cats make charming neutered pets. They play delightfully and are quite intelligent enough to know where their toys are kept. Ping-pong balls are a joy to them and if a Rex cat has a

A true aristocrat whose ancestors originated in the Far East: Seal-pointed Siamese

favourite cloth mouse you can put it on a side-table every morning and find it on the floor in the evening: the owner will have known exactly where to look for it. They are affectionate and make good 'lap-cats', although, like all felines, they curl up on their owner's knees whenever it suits them—not just when the owner invites them!

Their intelligence varies with the individual: there is a tale told of people who went out for the day and, on their return, found one of their Rex cats parading up and down in front of the house. She was clearly waiting for them and led them quickly to the top of the garden, where a stranger cat had treed their other Rex.

In view of the short time during which Rex have been known to us, hardly more, indeed, than 20 years, it is a tribute to their attractive dispositions and unusual appearance that they are already very much sought-after. In South Africa, in Australia and New Zealand, as well as in the USA and in Europe, these cats with the beautiful coats are being bred, winning at shows and becoming the loved pets of cat-owners all over the world.

Browned off

I must say it's a little hard,
Father left me here on guard,
Detailed to watch this flipping hole
While he goes for his evening stroll.

I mustn't doze, I mustn't stir
Or let out just a single purr.
A youngster *should* respect his pa,
But this is going rather far . . . .

Of all the soul-destroying chores—
Watching a hole that is not yours.

JANE ANTHONY

The Siamese

MARY DUNNILL

The Siamese cat is a beautiful, graceful creature with a long, lean body, a short close-lying coat, slim legs, dainty, spoon-shaped paws and a tapering whip-like tail. Its head is wedge-shaped with a long nose and flat skull; the ears are large, open at the base and pricked. Vivid blue eyes, oriental in shape with an inscrutable expression, make this a 'cat with a difference', mysterious and unusual. The characteristic feature is the coat pattern—that is the restriction of colour to the points. This is most striking in the seal-point Siamese cat, with its dark brown mask, ears, legs and tail contrasting with a creamy-fawn body colour.

The seal-point was the first to be imported into England in the 1880s and is still the most popular. Many of the imported cats carried genes for blue and chocolate and blue-pointed, chocolate-pointed and lilac-pointed Siamese cats were most certainly known many years before they were officially recognised and given breed numbers. It is possible to breed cats with the Siamese coat pattern in any colour known to felines today. We see red-points, cream-points, tabby-points, tortie-points and almost any combination of these colours such as blue tortie-tabby points—and so on *ad infinitum*—but so far green-points have eluded us!

In temperament the Siamese cat is a complete individualist; it is a devoted companion demanding love and attention, yet independent, wayward and often wicked. It is highly intelligent and readily trained. Sir Compton Mackenzie said 'an intelligent cat will be found in the house of the intelligent people. Siamese are the most intelligent of cats. They will tell you what they want. If you do not understand them, it is your fault, not theirs.' Human companionship is essential to their well-being; they like to be talked to and will enjoy carrying on a conversation with you. Their vocabulary is quite extensive, but the female in season excels all others. She becomes a shrieking banshee yelling for a mate.

Siamese cats will accompany you on a walk, some at your heel, while others like to run ahead and play hide and seek. They can be accustomed when young to a collar and lead and many enjoy a car ride. They will out-tire you at retrieving a ball of paper or similar plaything. My Tiannisomfun will play for hours tossing a piece of wire in the air, performing intricate ballet steps and is a joy to watch. One little cat had a favourite toy, a rabbit's foot which she would hide under a mat when she was tired of playing but she always remembered where to find it again.

Unless one has the proper facilities for breeding, it is best to have neutered cats. Siamese female cats can be very noisy in season and are very clever at opening doors and windows to escape. An entire male cat is impossible to keep in the house unless you have no sense of smell.

For perhaps a year the little pet tom may be all we could wish, but sooner or later he will take to roaming in search of sweethearts, staying away from his home so long as to give his fond owner cruel anxiety and returning a dissipated looking creature, probably bearing the marks of recent skirmishes with his rivals. When he comes back he is welcomed and forgiven as a prodigal should be, but a good meal and a sleep are all he cares about; he soon eludes the vigilance of his owner and disappears again, continuing this sort of life, with but little intermission until he is a mere wreck.

A pair of Siamese cats, either neutered males or spayed females or one of each sex is the ideal; they are much happier and much more fun in pairs and will not be lonely and miserable without you when left alone or boarded out on holiday.

Siamese kittens are born white, having lived in constant warmth until birth. Gradually faint colour develops on the extremities exposed to cooler air, the seal-points showing a dusky smudge on the nose and a dark pencil line on the edge of the ears. The dark brown of the seal-points is relatively quick to show but sometimes it is very difficult indeed to distinguish between lilac-points, chocolate-points and blue-points until they are about five or six weeks old. Sometimes the colour of the nose leather or paw pads will help one to decide, but this is not infallible. All the points should be the same shade of colour—a very difficult thing to achieve particularly with the chocolate-points and the red-points. Very often the ears show the correct colour and there is almost no colour at all on the front legs. Sometimes, with the lilac-points, the ears may be too blue or the tail too chocolate. The tabby-points may have a chocolate-tabby mask and ears and a non-matching seal-point ringed tail. However, it is only the show cat that needs to worry about these niceties for the character and lovableness of the cat is not affected by the non-matching points.

Siamese cats were once thought to be delicate and were treated as hot-house plants. This is wrong—they are as tough as any cat and will really enjoy playing in the snow or rain. It is as well, though, to give them a good rub down if they get wet. They do love warmth and will sit quite comfortably on a very hot radiator. The plate rack over my Aga is always occupied by one or more of my Siamese cats; sometimes four of them are curled up there, asleep and content. If, however, a Siamese cat is ill, then it seems more ill than any other cat. Be sure that your cat is given protection against the killer disease, feline infectious enteritis, by inoculation as a kitten and by booster inoculations as an adult cat. In the early days of cat shows, many cats and kittens succumbed to 'show fever'. There were no preventative inoculations known and treatment was very hit or miss. Three kittens arrived home from a show in 1929, were sick and had diarrhoea. They were given castor oil and anti-diarrhoea powders. After 15 days a vet was sent for and advised 'starve for one day and give starch in the food. Watch for sore throats.' Starch made the kittens worse. Two weeks later, there was still diarrhoea night and day. Advice from a fellow breeder was to stop all milk, give beef juice (brandy if necessary) and Nomis powders. A writer says:

> I gave the kittens scraped steak and poured the gravy from knuckle of veal, shank of mutton and two rabbits over a Madeira cake, added one tablespoonful of Brandy, mixed one Nomis powder in and the kittens took that. I am glad to say the kittens are all lively and full of mischief.
>
> (*Fur and Feather*, 1929)

This, of course, could not have been FIE, but what a wonderful cure in the days of plenty and no new pence.

Today our Siamese cats and kittens can be given protection against this disease. There are several vaccines for the purpose and we are apt to take this protection for granted, forgetting the hard work and research that goes into the finding. It is interesting to read that one of the veterinary surgeons present at the final meeting of the Feline Distemper Conference in 1934 said that future generations of veterinary surgeons and cat fanciers would have reason always to remember Mrs Duncan Hindley's name with great gratitude as being the person responsible for at least getting something done in the matter of feline distemper—'If a preventative is procured, Mrs Hindley deserves to have her name written in letters of gold at every cat show.' (*Fur and Feather*, 1934).

Siamese cats are splendid hunters. They will catch rabbits, mice and rats, stoats and snakes and, regrettably, birds. I was horrified, one day, to see one of my Siamese queens carrying a white pigeon nearly as big as herself through my pantry window, tripping over the wings as she walked. There is an amusing story of the Siamese cat who used to eat cheese and then go and breathe down mouse-holes to lure them out. They are also thieves but at least they are honest about it and will snatch a morsel from the fork on its way to your mouth from the plate. Samiha can open my pantry door: she lies on her side and pulls it open with her paw and all the other cats troop in and help themselves unless I am within earshot and hear the click of the latch. My first Siamese, Becky, in Stratford-upon-Avon, brought home a whole oxheart and put it in her usual feeding dish before attempting to eat any. She had negotiated a high fence, jumped onto a thatched roof and gone in to the next cottage through a bedroom window to get the heart and had carried it in her mouth out again from the window, down the thatched roof, and over the fence. I watched her waddling up the garden path, bumping it as she went. Minna, my blue-point, would not come in one evening and I found her in the garden, quietly consuming someone's evening meal, a perfectly luscious shoulder of lamb. I never knew whose it was and I dared not enquire.

Siamese are very photogenic, the seal-points particularly so, their beautiful blue eyes peering out of their little brown faces making an immediate impact; their grace and elegance are a joy but endless patience and ingenuity are needed to catch them before they walk out of your sight. Cats and kittens are to be seen in all kinds of advertisements, on greetings cards, on chocolate boxes, biscuit tins, wallpapers, fabrics and, best of all, in the many superb collections of photographs in colour and black and white in the spate of cat books published in recent years. Tabby-points make spectacular pictures, especially when photographed in natural surroundings and in movement. One can imagine the tiger hunting in the jungle.

All the 'best' Siamese cats have a long whip-like tail but many people think a kink is an attraction and one of the characteristics of the breed. I had a male seal-point, Hamlet, with a beautiful head but a double kink in his tail. He heard me say so often 'a beautiful cat spoilt by his tail' that he became quite self-conscious and would sit down on his tail so that the kink could not be seen. We used to call him the foreman because he would trot to and fro to make quite sure we were working hard when gardening. Sir Compton Mackenzie liked the kink—'Stumps had a short tail with a double kink like my beloved first Sylvia' – and whenever he visited the Siamese Cat Club shows to present the rosettes, he always deplored the present-day endeavours to eliminate the kink and the squint. Hetty Gray Baker has similar feelings. 'If Siamese cats in Siam have round heads, eyes that are crossed and tails that are kinked, why, then that is a Siamese cat.'

There are several legends about the kinked tail. A Siamese princess, bathing in a stream, slipped her rings on her cat's tail. For safety, the cat crooked her tail and Siamese cats' tails have been kinked over since. Then there was the pair of cats searching in a wood for the sacred goblet which had been stolen from the temple. When they found it, the little queen twisted her tail round the stem of the goblet and remained guarding it while the husband cat went off to report the find. Several days passed and when the husband returned, five kittens had been born, all with kinks in their tails, so ever after, Siamese cats have a kink at the end of their tail.

Not only is the kink frowned upon today, but the squint also. I like a slight squint, giving the oriental look, but permanently crossed eyes do not find favour on the show bench. The desired almond-shaped eye, slanting towards the nose is becoming somewhat of a rarity—perhaps that too is being bred out by careless selection of breeding stock. The blue eyes of the Siamese cat and its unusual coat pattern are the characteristics which make this 'cat with a difference'. Some white Persian cats and some white shorthair breeds have blue eyes but no other domestic cat has the bright blue expressive eyes of the Siamese cat.

The earliest Siamese cats known in England were exhibited at the Crystal Palace Show in 1871 and were described as 'unnatural, nightmare kind of cats'. In the 1800s several pairs were sent from Siam; the famous Pho and Mia were among the first to be named in the Siamese Cat Club register and have sometimes been called the Adam and Eve of the British Siamese Cat Fancy. Until the imposition of the quarantine rule in 1928, a considerable number of cats were imported. In the early days these cats were slow to get acclimatised, they were treated as hot-house plants and few survived for more than two or three years. However the Siamese cat of today is as hardy as any; like all cats, they love warmth and sunshine but will play happily in the snow. Some reach a wonderfully old age. Recently I visited a spayed female, happily awaiting her 21st birthday in a few weeks' time or 147 years in human time —an incredible age! I have known several Siamese cats live to be 18 or 19 years of age but 12 years is a good average. Show cats are generally at their best at about 2 years old; the males have matured but have not yet become 'jowly' and most queens improve and look their best with pregnancy.

If, after reading all this, you decide to have a Siamese cat, you must make up your mind that henceforward you cannot call your soul your own; you will inevitably spoil it because it will demand to be spoilt. If you are sitting comfortably in a chair, you must get up and open the door for the cat to go out. Two minutes later, the cat will rattle the door handle to be let in again. If you are reading, the cat will sit down on just that piece you are trying to read. If you are writing, the cat will chew your pen until you have to give up. If you are eating, your Siamese will demand the most toothsome piece. If you are walking, your cat will weave round your ankles and if you should trip over the cat, you will apologise to her for being clumsy enough to do so and not suggest that she is at fault. If you are relaxing, there is no better way than with a sleeping cat on your lap. Your Siamese cat will love you with a deep, possessive love and you will be her slave.

All cats express their feelings vocally to a greater or less extent but none approach the Siamese in either the variety or the volume of the sounds they produce. The Siamese voice is pitched in a higher key and some cat lovers, used to the plaintive mew, find what they call the Siamese yowl unattractive. But for Siamese lovers, the extraordinary range and freedom of the voice, from a hoarse croak of pleasure to a modulated wiaouwwau of protest, is music. Perhaps it is an acquired taste; Siamese have a unique language of their own, and use their voices not only to draw attention to the approach of meal time, but to comment on anything and nothing. Some Siamese talk more than others, but all talk much more than other cats.

SIDNEY AND HELEN DENHAM, *The Siamese Cat*

3
Cats in the Wild

Wild cats threatened by Man

JANET BARBER

In the past man has seldom used nature's resources intelligently or sparingly and for the most part the exploitation of the wild cats for their furs, for example, has continued without people wincing with horror at the way in which a species is killed, or worrying about the time when there will no longer be any more whales, turtles, antelopes or spotted cats.

It is only in the last decade that man has become more reflective about the uses to which he puts the animal kingdom and the abuses he inflicts on it. One of the ways in which one can now engage people's interest is to point out that there is an immediate danger of many species of animals, birds and plants becoming extinct, all of which are of great benefit to man in a variety of ways. Man will be the loser if wild species disappear. It is in his interest to retain them as vital parts of the natural world. People are sometimes unimpressed when one explains just how threatened crocodiles or perhaps turtles are. However the first plays a vital and unusual part in the ecological balance of rivers and lakes all over the world and the second would be a valuable source of protein for people if managed properly. Whales or wild cats stir the imagination more easily. They seem larger, more vulnerable perhaps and are nearer relatives of man. The exploitation of both seems senseless and exceptionally cruel. The wild cats of the world, as a group, probably hold more fascination for people than any other—a close second would possibly be the great apes.

Extravagantly beautiful, inhabiting the most remote parts of the globe the tigers, leopards and cheetahs, in spite of their traditional ferocity, are highly vulnerable. Partly because of their great beauty, their fierceness and their need for large areas in which to live, wild cats are among the most threatened animals in the world. Undoubtedly the exploitation, which even now continues to intensify, of these species for their fur has been the major factor contributing to their decline. Another reason for their plummeting numbers is the widespread destruction of their habitat. The tropical grasslands of Africa, the swamps and forests of Asia and the lowland jungles of the Latin American tropics are coming under inexorable pressure as rising human populations demand ever more land. The cutting into of these virgin areas is continuing at a horrifying rate and any species that either threatens man or can provide him with an unexpected financial bonus as he invades the remaining wild areas of the world, stands no chance—and it is not just the spotted cats which are suffering in this way. Man it seems will never learn to co-operate with, or even tolerate, nature rather than compete with it and exterminate certain elements in it for ever.

One of the most unpleasant aspects of the capture of species for their fur is the great cruelty involved. Methods are haphazard and ruthless. In Africa leopards are trapped alive and killed with a hot poker to avoid the skin being marked; in South America hunters may take up to a week or longer to collect the animals which will have taken some while to die in a vicious leghold trap. However, if women intent on wearing the coats of these species are unmoved by the miseries of their capture, one can hardly expect the trappers to be sensitive people. Until more humane methods of capture can be devised for the trapping of wild creatures, the use of wild animals for the fur trade should be stopped. The wastage is also enormous and the trapping patterns completely unscientific as one large area after another, whether it is in South America or the savannah country of Africa, is often completely cleared of cats, creating a great imbalance of species. A major prey animal like a tiger or a leopard controls populations of deer or wild pig or rats; once they are removed their prey can multiply uncontrollably to the detriment of human populations and their crops. If it could be established that there were enough snow leopards or tiger cats, for example, to enable a certain number to be used for the fur trade and that a certain number could be taken without upsetting nature's delicate balance this would be acceptable, provided of course that the method of capture was sufficiently humane. Such a scheme would enable the exploitation to be done on a rational basis and would, perhaps, ensure the survival of the species as a valuable resource. It would also of course enable the countries involved to gain a proper income from this wildlife resource. But until it can be established that a population of fur-bearing creatures can withstand cropping, trapping should cease. The Australian Government has recently taken this line and is preventing the export of kangaroos until it has been proved the species as a whole can support a carefully judged amount of exploitation.

Unfortunately there is everything to indicate that few wild cats should be used by the fur trade at this time. Numbers of nearly all species are declining far too quickly and perhaps have already reached a stage from which recovery will be impossible.

Undoubtedly the most famous and most threatened of the world's large cats is the tiger, once referred to as 'a great-hearted gentleman'. They have suffered disastrously in the last 30 years. In the 1940s there were probably as many as 40,000 in India but a recent census conducted by the India Forestry Service revealed there were now only 1,827 tigers remaining. The other seven races of tiger are also threatened with extinction and number little more than 3,000 in total. In Java there may be about five tigers, in Sumatra perhaps a few more. The Bali tiger, from the romantic island of the same name, may well be extinct and the Caspian tiger just manages to survive in the damp lowlands around the Caspian Sea. The Siberian tiger, the largest of the tigers, is very thinly distributed over a large area and the Indo-Chinese race, of which there may be about 2,000 individuals, is struggling to survive in the recently war-torn countries of East Asia. The Chinese tiger is not much better placed and his skin is usually available for sale in the shops in Peking. Although the spectacular tiger shikars held in the jungles of India during Queen Victoria's reign and later, perhaps had some effect on tiger populations, by far the most serious threats have come with the commercial exploitation of the tiger for skins and trophies, the felling of the jungle for timber and the reclamation of swamps. The tiger is also often declared a man-eater but the accusation is usually unjustified. Like all animals the tiger is most reluctant to approach human beings and it is only if he is injured (probably by man) or is too old to hunt his normal prey that he will approach humans. A recent survey showed that man-eaters constitute a minute percentage of the tigers found in India.

The tiger has a large range depending how available are its prey species and, as jungle is cleared, whole natural systems disappear together with the least adaptable and most magnificent of the creatures it supports. The World Wildlife Fund has launched, together with the Indian government, a massive campaign to save the tiger in India. Some suitable reserve areas already exist but other areas with good-sized tiger populations will also be declared reserves. The Indian and Pakistan governments have now banned all hunting of the tiger and the export of tiger skins.

The leopard in Asia is widely distributed but declining for the same reasons as the tiger. It does kill domestic stock when its own prey is scarce and for this reason it is hunted also. The cheetah has now been extinct in India, where it was used to hunt gazelles, since the 1950s. It has always been less resilient than the leopard. There are probably a number of cheetahs in Iran; if they do exist, they would be the only ones surviving outside Africa. Probably the two rarest spotted cats in Asia are the snow leopard and the clouded leopard. Both have exceptionally beautiful coats. The snow leopard has pale creamy fur with long silky guard hairs and faintly brown wide-spaced spots. The clouded leopard has a deep-golden coat with a large chocolate-squared design. The snow leopard has a wide range through the Himalayas just below the snow line and central Asia and lives a lonely and remote existence. Nevertheless man has penetrated his mountainous and often snowy habitat to reduce his numbers to about 400. The World Wildlife Fund is helping with the establishment of a reserve in the hills of Pakistan, for the snow leopard and other rare species, where it is suspected that the snow leopard is killed less for the value of its pelt than the desire on the part of local people to kill any predator at all. The clouded leopard has an even

A Brown Tabby shorthair, with typical British type, one of the oldest
varieties known

A very promising Sealpoint Siamese kitten at seven months old

wider range throughout South-East Asia and its richly patterned coat has a high market value. It won't be long before many smaller species in Asia—which resemble alarmingly our own domestic cat —like the marbled cat and the jungle cat are threatened as the larger species become harder to find. The World Wildlife Fund, has, with the help of the International Fur Trade Federation, conducted a survey of leopard and cheetah populations throughout Africa. In spite of increasing efforts on the part of African governments to control the illegal trade in skins across the often unpoliced boundaries of their countries, the pressure on spotted cats is unremitting.

The cheetah is the fastest mammal on land and can reach speeds of nearly 70 miles an hour. This graceful cat is declining and probably numbers less than 2,000 in Africa's national parks but unless the areas of parks can be extended or buffer zones created there will not be room for species like the cheetah, rhinos and elephants to manoeuvre and even those protected will be threatened by lack of space and over-crowding. The cheetah, unlike the leopard, cannot combat pressure on its numbers and cubs appear to be dying of disease and malnutrition. Cheetahs are easily driven off prey once they have killed and often have to kill several times before eating sufficient. There are between 5,000 and 10,000 leopards in Africa's parks and, although more resilient than the cheetah, will not for long be able to sustain the hunting pressure. In addition, however, there are several severely endangered sub-species—the Somali leopard, for example, which has a skin with unusually small fine spots and for this reason is much in demand. There is also the Barbary leopard which is found in the north of the African continent but has little chance of surviving.

In 1968 and 1969 the United States imported over 17,000 leopard skins, which is equivalent to cleaning out 200,000 square miles of the best leopard country in Africa. The 3,000-odd cheetah skins imported into the United States in the same period would account for the cheetahs found, at the highest density, in over 100,000 square miles of Africa. The rate at which jaguars, the third largest cat after the tiger and lion, are disappearing from the South American jungles presents another horrifying statistic; an area of 40,000 square miles a year is being cleared of this richly patterned creature. The jaguar is found in the tropical lowland forest of Latin American countries and these are the areas now under greatest pressure for development. The forests are

F

being cleared for grazing chiefly and, as humans move in, the jaguar is the first target for them as its trail is not too difficult to follow, its pelt valuable and it may pose a threat to newly introduced cattle. Several Latin American countries have banned all dealing in jaguar skins but the trade continues.

For ocelots the picture is no better and even greater numbers than jaguar are exported. Ocelots live higher up and are more nocturnal but this isn't preventing their decline. Hunters clear large areas and move further into the interior for the larger species. As they become scarce the smaller species like the delicate margay, tiger cat and Geoffrey's cat are taken. It is an impossible task to explain the recklessness of the exploitation to those responsible, even though they will have exhausted this resource soon. The natural heritage argument won't take one much further either when a few jaguar or margay pelts will earn as much income as a year's back-breaking labour. The construction of the Trans-Amazonian highway is wrecking the fragile tropical ecosystem of the Brazilian jungle, one of the oldest and most vulnerable in the world. Here again, the cats and innumerable other species are being exterminated or driven into the most remote parts of the jungle interior.

Brazil has prohibited all dealings in wildlife products but, as one expert said recently, it is hardly surprising if the chasing of contraband jaguar skins over a country five times the size of western Europe ranks low on the priorities of the police. Therefore countries at the receiving end of the trade should produce their own legislation dovetailing with the laws of countries struggling to stop the trade. However, governments in the countries providing markets may only be moved to stop the import of threatened species and their products if the electorate is vociferous enough. The United States now has an Endangered Species Act which prohibits the import of skins and the products of an increasing number of species into America. This is the most far-reaching legislation so far introduced by any country. The US government appears to act quickly, keeping up with trends in the exploitation of threatened species. Recently several more spotted cats were added to the prohibited list, including jaguar, ocelot, margay and tiger cat. The fur trade has often been referred to as the second oldest profession. It is also by tradition, one of the most secretive. However, in the last two or three years it has shown itself prepared to cooperate with conservationists in attempts to prevent the extinction of, especially, the wild cats.

In 1969 the West German furriers agreed not to fashion the skins of endangered cats and this undertaking was followed by the furriers of New York.

The British Fur Trade Association and the International Fur Traders Federation reached an agreement in 1970 with the International Union for the Conservation of Nature and the World Wildlife Fund and placed a voluntary ban on the use of tiger, snow and clouded leopard skins and the skins of two very rare species of otter, the gaint and La Plata otters of South America. This was an important step forward and even more so as a temporary ban was imposed on the use of cheetah skins until a survey had been done to establish just how threatened the species was.

While many furriers were clearly going to cooperate with the ban, others made it quite plain publicly that they had no intention of observing the restrictions and were seen, on television in Britain, standing in warehouses full of spotted cat skins.

The British government finally made a long-awaited move in March 1972 and made it illegal to import into Britain the skins of tiger, snow and clouded leopards. However, the authorities were not prepared to forbid the use of the beautiful and threatened South American otters but did restrict the import into this country of cheetah and leopard skins, making it necessary for the skins to be stamped by the British trade mission in the country of origin.

With the successful completion of a new convention prohibiting the trading in many of the world's threatened species, including a large number of wild cats, there is increased hope for their survival. This meeting, held in Washington in February 1973, was attended by 80 nations who agreed on a convention which effectively bars dealing in about 400 species of threatened mammals, birds, reptiles and fish. However, even if international conventions or laws protecting cats are agreed upon and introduced, people will always flout or break them. A famous New York furrier was recently prosecuted and fined $20,000 for illegally possessing a wide range of threatened fur-bearing mammal skins, including those of the cheetah, leopard, jaguar and ocelot.

Efficient protection of species such as these in the grasslands or jungles of the world in national parks offers the best hope for their long-term survival. However governments in the countries where the animals live should be given every encouragement and support by the developed countries which provide the markets and which must prevent their import and display in cities such as New York, Paris, London and Rome.

My experiences with Scottish wildcats

GRAHAME DANGERFIELD

I have kept most wild British mammals for 20 years. In the begin-ing, once I had established groups of foxes, badgers, and even a baby grey seal, it was natural to look to the rarer British mammals —the otter, the pine marten and, especially, the Scottish wildcat. At that time those three species were rarely kept in captivity— indeed to this day very few zoos or private collections have them. In the case of the wildcat, it had not then been bred in captivity in Britain since 1884 and, so far as I know, that was the only British captive-breeding.

The *International Zoo Yearbook* in 1961 reported captive births of the European wildcat (a species as good as identical to ours) in Switzerland and Yugoslavia. If one discounts the British 1884 record, then these two, certainly among those people with whom I was in contact in the wildlife field, were as good as 'world firsts', an expression commonly used by zoo people. For many reasons, especially the challenge of captive-breeding, this was a species that I very much wanted.

Years passed and I went on wanting. I asked people in Scotland to help, I advertised extensively—nothing. In 1962 my luck changed, very suddenly. As is often the case, a chance meeting produced results. My brother had some friends at our house, among them a most attractive nurse from Scotland. I jokingly asked her to get hold of some wildcat kittens and phone me when she had got them. Unknown to me, she went home, wrote an article in a local paper and a gamekeeper contacted her to say he had three kittens, their eyes still closed—the ideal age for bottle-rearing and I hoped therefore, taming. For another great challenge was the old, old story that this was the most untamable animal in the world—pound for pound the fiercest thing alive; as the years passed, what nonsense that all proved to be.

As soon as I received the news that the kittens had been found my feet never touched the ground. I flew to Scotland at once and flew back home with them the same day.

I had two main worries—could I bottle-rear them with complete success and were they real wildcats? I was lucky with the former, for we had not long before reared a domestic kitten from day old to see how we would get on. This was not just an experiment, for it was born to a mother who could never rear a kitten. We reared it—very badly in my opinion—but we recorded every step most carefully, so we had a 'rearing blueprint' to apply to the wildcat kittens. The latter was perhaps a greater worry.

My kittens had been found in Perth, at that time about as far south as their range extended. The wildcat used to roam all England and Scotland (but possibly never Ireland). Even before World War I, however, it was driven back to dangerously low numbers in wild areas of Scotland only. In 1962 its numbers were for the first time in many years starting to pick up and the population was starting to spread a little but even so I feared Perth might be a little too far south and while I did not suspect that we had feral or wild-reared domestic kittens, I did fear very much that we might have a litter of mixed parentage. That is to say one true wildcat and one feral or 'domestic, gone wild' cat.

At that time Professor Amoroso of the Royal Veterinary College was interested in cats and he advised we rear the kittens on cow's milk. This surprised me, since we were using a lot of Ostermilk on animals like fox cubs with fairly good results. I felt these terribly important kittens ought to have something with more in it than cow's milk but I am not a technical man, so followed the advice I had been given. The kittens did well and all lived. Probably today more is known about cat's milk in general and perhaps today one would act differently.

The risk of death from feline enteritis was very high indeed. The kittens were reared with a pipette and a bicycle valve rubber was jammed on the end as a sort of teat. They were placed on a clean towel for every feed and weighed several times a day in grammes. A chart was kept for each kitten and a graph was plotted several times a day. This was compared with the progress bulletin we already had for the domestic kitten; the wildcat kittens did better but they had much more attention. Every single item that they came into contact with was kept under sterilised liquid between every feed. The kittens lived in a room away from other animals and every possible precaution was taken to see they did not get exposed to any infection before they could receive their injections against feline enteritis. Faeces samples were collected frequently and, if I remember correctly, worms were not found, which was unusual. We know with other species that worms, or a heavy worm burden, plus bottle-rearing can very easily equal death but it is not difficult, if one knows the worms are there, to eradicate them early and so avoid all trouble.

While the kittens were still very young, before they could see, we placed a dead sparrow in the cage—the reaction was instant, incredible and reassuring. In a second all the kittens were fighting and growling amongst themselves, fights so serious that one could have been forgiven for thinking injury might result. A sparrow per kitten was then given and each kitten dragged its sparrow to an opposite corner of the cage, hissing and growling, and barging against any other kitten that came near. By this time splendid markings were appearing on the kittens' coats and the thick black-ringed tails were making the final point—if any point were needed after the sparrow incident—these really were true Scottish wildcats, just as the gamekeeper had assured me at the very beginning. He had seen their mother, killed by dogs, but when we walked out into the hills so that I could examine the body, the hooded crows and, the gamekeeper said, the buzzards, had taken it off. The den I did see and some very convincing adult wildcat hair on a rock but I had still feared I might have half-breeds. Now I was happy I had not.

The kittens were weaned without problem and every meal was wild game : pheasant, rabbit, hare, odd small birds—and very little else. They grew well and had magnificent coats and, remarkably, they loved and daily played with my large Alsatian. They had of course by that time had all their injections. They outgrew their cage quickly and were given a small room in the house. This was almost a porch, with tiled floor, and was easy to clean. Then we noticed another new thing—the cats (as they now were) would never dig a hole in anything to pass a motion : an earth tray or any other kind of tray was a waste of time. It was easy in those days just to open the door to their room and let them into my office but as time passed it became necessary to let them live out of doors and so a converted shed was planned. Up to this time they were still playing with the dog and with me and would leap lovingly to my shoulder as soon as I entered the room, where they would stand like domestic tabbies and rub themselves against my neck—they were in fact much more affectionate than most domestic cats. At feeding time this would change and each cat would vanish growling to a distant corner with its own whole wild rabbit and at that time would have probably scratched and attacked any intruder.

As tiny kittens—but only after the injections were complete—the cats had appeared on television in a London studio. When they were just on full grown they went again and took the journey extremely well. Once out of the travelling basket, they climbed at once to my shoulders and would not leave me. When the time came therefore to move them to the converted shed, no one visualised any problem at all and we carried them there in armfuls without any trouble. Naturally in a totally strange place they were nervous, and explored every corner as though it were going to bite, with that typical cat reaction to something not understood, low posture, worried eyes, muscles tense to spring in any direction. I stayed with them for some time to see them in as it were but one must remember we were now dealing with full-grown animals and the 'parent-bond' that I may have had with them should by now have been well passed.

From the moment this home change occurred the cats were never quite the same. They would still rush to greet me and leap on to my shoulders as I arrived but they would not stay long with me. In a short time they would come to me only to collect food from my hand and, as explained, once they had food, they would leave me and become aggressive to me, each other, indeed the world. To maintain a constant supply of natural food (rabbit and hare almost always) we had now purchased an old Land-Rover and had it completely converted for night shooting. Not only did the cats have their own car therefore but also their own deep freeze, where their own food supply was kept. Night shooting from the Land-Rover on a friend's farm was now an almost nightly event.

I will never know exactly why the final behaviour change came about. I will always believe it was the home change, something I have seen all too often with several animals of this size. I now firmly believe that, if at all possible, a cage should be designed to cope with an animal growing up, right from the start. By this I mean one allows the animal into the new area by stages, or best by opening a connecting door—a sudden move with a full-grown but still young animal can 'detame' very quickly.

One day I went out to the cats and observed mating, or at least attempted mating. From that day on the cats' behaviour to me changed completely, although by this time they were none too friendly anyway. They were now about 10 months old. Soon after this came a bitter, bitter blow; the *remains* of one cat was found one morning—the other two cats resented my presence very much.

I at once sent off what was left of the body to my old and trusted friend, David Blackmore, now Professor. He is a veterinary pathologist. He could find nothing wrong with the material I had sent him. The dead cat was male. We knew we had two males and one female at the start.

It was finally decided that there had been a fight to the death. Sexual maturity had been witnessed and 'anti-parent' behaviour to me had been observed. It would seem that with no warning the two males had decided to sort it out between themselves. The loser had been partly eaten. All this is of course supposition—the cat may have died for some odd reason, although I would have thought Blackmore would have found something if it had and the body could have been eaten by rats—but all this seems most unlikely. I cannot see any rat lasting five minutes, indeed five seconds, in a wildcat cage.

The cats would still take food from my hand; in fact if I held a dead rabbit high they would leap to it, hang on and not let go until I dropped the rabbit. They would therefore approach me every day at feeding time, a state of partial tameness one could argue, but it was now quite impossible to pick them up. We now decided that there was no question at all about the genuineness of the breed—they had turned totally wild. They now had short tails with massive blunt tips—the tip was the thickest part of the tail in fact. It was nice to know that the wildcat had finally been tamed, albeit for only ten months but it did show it could be done and this was probably the first time it had ever been done. I felt satisfied with that side of the project.

The time had now come to look at the final target: to breed, for the first time in Britain since 1884 and for the third time in the world, in captivity. I had now lost interest in the converted shed. It was ugly, the roof was none too safe and an escape might occur one day, and it was 'un-wildcattish'—just a shed, not a habitat.

The garden had a wild and woolly pine forest, small but very forest-like: thick, dense, with that pleasing floor of pine needles that seems to produce a soundless environment. A large and expensive cage was planned. No one entered the wood, so the wildcats would have complete security. The area looked right and felt right and it is by feeling something that I have bred many animals in my life that others have failed with.

Sadly because of cost, which is so often the case, it was finally decided not to have trees in the cage. There were two ways of having them in it. One was to roof the whole wood and to do this with wildcat-proof netting would probably have cost many hundreds of pounds. The other alternative, to run the roof netting up to and around a tree trunk was certainly possible but I feared that sooner or later that dangerous joining point, as the wind blew and the years passed, would come away slightly and a cat would climb a tree, and squeeze out where the netting had started to come away. I will always regret deciding not to do this, since I now feel it could have been done with total security.

The final cage was very nice, with an excellent double door, padlocks on both, and a huge and wonderful den, with two sections and two entrances. The cats were taken to this area in a cage and released into it. They liked it. With pine trees all around they now looked superb but this final move was also the final step in de-taming and they now became wild to the point of almost hurting themselves in their attempts to get out of one's way. They would still creep forward and leap to a rabbit in my hand but only very resentfully. If they were in the den and one opened the door to look at them, they would explode out of the box in an alarming way, alarming in case they hurt themselves but also alarming because each time they missed my face by inches and cursed and swore as they shot past me.

Attempts were made to disturb them as little as possible. In the spring of 1963 we hoped for a birth—there was no evidence that the Scottish wildcat should take longer to mature than an ordinary cat. Both animals now had massive coats and they looked so well that even uninitiated visitors remarked on their condition. It was easy to read pregnancy into this condition with each passing day— surely that one looks a little fatter than the other? Surely it looks fatter than last week? Surely it is always the fat one that is in the box? But nothing happened. Sad but confident that the wildcat takes longer to mature than the domestic we ran through until June, when wildcats breed. But nothing happened.

June 1964—a year later—the same questions, the same statements. Again nothing happened. Mixed with a sad feeling of defeat were worrying questions now: are we certain that two years ago when the animals were tiny kittens, we sexed them correctly? Are we certain the animal which died in the fight was male? We began to believe the female must have died and we had two males left. The wildcat is fluffy-bottomed and hard to sex when adult—I ended up on the ground with the vet beside me, lying there like idiots trying to see under the cats' tails. We could see nothing and gave up. A plan was made to net them and check the sex but I was frightened of injury or some terrible and extreme stress and abandoned the idea. I was fairly sure now that we had two males and hopes of breeding faded away.

At about this time my father died. Mother was forced to sell our house and land for development. My eight-year TV series ended too at this time. Perhaps the greatest tragedy of my life, I was compelled to scrap my whole collection. The foreign species went mostly to friends I knew would look after them. The British section, by far the biggest group I had, went to the local council as a gift. They started what was meant to be a conservation education collection of British wildlife only but unfortunately it did not take them long to start aviaries of racing pigeons and cages of spiny mice and so on and the place became just another small zoo, with no complete British wildlife theme. Conservation education it seemed to me had been completely overlooked.

However the wildcats had a reasonable cage with an attractive den but not the sort of den that could be easily supervised should breeding ever happen. I left for Africa not long after this, and became a warden in the Serengeti National Park, Tanzania. I had the happiest time of my life in this massive 6,000-square-mile wildlife paradise. I spent a lot of time making sound recordings, which resulted in my record 'Sounds of the Serengeti'.

I had been in the Serengeti about a year when a rumour reached me that the wildcats had bred in the council zoo but the babies had been lost. I was amazed this had happened and immediately put the age of sexual maturity at about three years. I was wrong. I wrote at once to the zoo for more information but had no reply to my letter, which did not surprise me. A year later I returned to Britain and the first thing I did was visit the zoo to find out what had happened. The story that emerged filled me with horror and anger.

One day kittens had been found. Thinking the mother cat would not rear them, they had taken them from her. No effort, so far as I could make out, had been made to decide what would be done with regard to bottle-rearing and no definite information—again so far as I could gather—had been obtained that it was necessary to remove the litter at all. All the kittens perished quickly. Not long after this the mother died and alone and restless, it was only a few weeks before the father died too. And that was how the most important captive animal chapter of my life had finally ended. Post mortems, as I recall, on the adults had shown a heavy worm burden but presumably there had been no worm checks from faeces samples after I went abroad—a vital animal husbandry step that should be taken all the time—and presumably feline enteritis injection boosts had also been ignored. The cause of death therefore was not established.

Part of the reason I had donated my collection (eight years of my life) to the council was that every possible effort should be made to breed from the stock I had given. On my return from Africa I found that the ravens had not even been given a place to build a nest. After weeks of pressure a platform was finally put up but I had to drive over and personally set up the nest; the raven laid eggs a week later, possibly a first for Britain. The eggs came to nothing. Soon after a raven had a cough—symptom of a dangerous lung-worm that is easily treated. I urged repeatedly that this be dealt with but my advice was ignored and the bird died, thus breaking a vitally important breeding pair. It went on like this, and my great hopes of taking up my breeding studies again where I had left off about three years before were quickly dashed. I gave up, feeling the council would be only too delighted if I did.

And so it was that in early 1968 I started all over again. Foxes, badgers, grey squirrels and countless others were bottle-reared from tiny babies and a whole new collection was started with animals that I hoped, because of hand-rearing, would be completely tame and would therefore breed.

I wrote once again to every wildcat contact I could think of but drew a complete blank as expected. I even tracked down the game-keeper who had helped six years before but he could not help me. Eyes-closed kittens would probably never happen again anyway. Pressure was maintained on sources of wildcats for the next four years—there was not even a small crack in the dam.

Suddenly in 1971 a new gamekeeper in Scotland, much further north this time, got hold of three kittens that were well weaned. They arrived by rail, filthy, in a dangerously airless box—I think they were lucky to get through at all. A male and two females, he had said, so we were off to a good start. But would these wild and mad little spitfires ever settle enough to breed? Any attempt to win friendship was a complete waste of time and we also feared that after their dreadful journey a full belly, peace and quiet and a thorough worming were what was needed. Faeces were taken at once and worms were found in heavy numbers. A few days' rest and quiet and we found they cleaned themselves up well and looked very good. Now we went ahead with the vital feline enteritis in-jections, a time with a wild animal that always gets me very much on edge but there was no problem. During the very thick-gloved handling this required we carried out a sex check and received a bitter blow. Every kitten was male. I have learnt over the years that one is likely to be told the sex of *any* animal wrongly, by either the previous owners or finders. The battle now was to get them as fit as possible and breeding was forgotten about.

Weeks passed and the mad little kittens, with great care and more worming, grew into three simply magnificent animals—much bigger than the ones I had bottle-raised. Suddenly another phone call came from the same gamekeeper—another wildcat, this time definitely female, had been caught in a gin trap. It was a young animal and its foot was hurt. This one came down by rail in a much better box. Immediately on its arrival, with bated breath, we sexed the animal: *male again.* Our luck was out.

I called the vet again and he came at once. He took one look at the cat and said it must be destroyed. In terms of breeding—the all important purpose of this exercise—this did not matter. But it was a plucky cat with a nice big face. Could anything be done? It was finally decided after a lot of thought and soul searching that the leg, if amputated at the shoulder, might stop the infection that was raging. The animal had been injured in this vile trap many days before and I had not known this. Thank God the gin trap is now illegal in England but when will Scotland do something about their law on this subject?

I made the point that to amputate at the shoulder might well render this cat unable to copulate, for gripping the female with both front paws might I felt be important. Another big rethink took place. Finally the vet decided to have a go. The whole leg was reset and two sections of damaged bone removed. We took every possible care with this animal and to everybody's surprise it came through, with a first-class, although slightly short, front leg. The vet could not believe it had worked. Wormed and injected it grew into a fine cat.

We now sat back with four large male wildcats, the three brothers kept together, the injured one alone, and wondered what would happen next. John Buxton was filming here and he put me in touch with a man he knew in Scotland who might help. As luck would have it, not long after this, the man's terriers cornered a kitten in a drainpipe and it was sent to us. It had many small injuries on its face but with care and treatment these disappeared.

And it was a *female*.

Aware of the fight to the death years before, we decided the presence of a female with the three brothers might cause trouble and start another fight. She went to live with 'Broken-leg' and they were happy together. She had been born a little late in the year and I feared this might mean she had domestic blood in her but her behaviour in the next few months made us believe this was highly unlikely.

It had been argued that wildcats, if pure, should breed May/June, once a year. One authority argues that a second litter in August occurs, while others argue this happens only if there is domestic blood in the animal. We will always worry about this but I think in time we may prove this right or wrong with our studies here.

Time passed and all the cats grew into superb adults. Now we had a problem. The three brothers ought perhaps to have a cage each to completely rule out any serious fighting. We could not afford three really good cages and I was faced with the very regrettable decision that two of the brothers would have to go. One was sent off to a wildlife park in Cumberland and I cannot remember ever parting with an animal that I wanted to keep more. He was absolutely magnificent and the best of the three. He had to go because he was fractionally more restless than the others—if breeding one day were to be tried, then only the most stable cats should remain. I had a great personal attachment to him and it really hurt to box him up and send him off but money compels these things. The two brothers that remained got on well—but how long would it last?

Now Philip Wayre at the Norfolk Wildlife Park bred a litter. In due course he had a surplus female and wanted an extra male—we did a swop. The only trouble was that he had bred from a Scottish wildcat and a European wildcat, so a half-breed female came to me. I say half-breed but of course the Scottish and European races are scientifically extremely similar but the Wayre female was a much smaller, paler animal, with a rather worrying tail—not the massive thick tail I like to see. However, she soon settled down and the remaining cat of the three brothers liked her. They wintered together without incident and Broken-leg and his wild little wife wintered in another cage. Still suspicious that wildcats might take two years or more to reach sexual maturity—and not knowing how long Philip Wayre had taken to breed them—we sat back and waited for time to pass. Also, as they were not tame, we feared they might never breed.

We all got very excited therefore when on 27 April 1972, the Wayre female was seen being mated and again a week later on 4 May. We hoped but did not really believe that she had conceived. On 15 May Broken-leg was seen to be trying to mate but the female broke away.

Excitement rose yet higher when the Wayre female on 25 June, at the right time of year, looked pregnant. This excitement was soon to die when on 6 July there was no litter and she just looked, we decided, fat. The significance of 6 July was that that was the date on which nine weeks had elapsed between the last observed mating. (It was felt at that time that wildcat gestation was 63 days and the domestic cat around 58 days.) We allowed one extra week and on 12 July she still looked just fat but we had an entry in our 'Births and Behaviour' book which read 'Wayre female looking very big, and that was on 7 July. Not knowing what to expect or believe, and not daring to hope for too much, when the Wayre female was not seen in the pen on 14 July, I very slowly opened her nestbox lid a fraction and I am sure my heart just stopped for seconds on end while I watched her lying there with what looked like three kittens beside her. A vitally important bonus was that she did not seem to mind this peep into her nursery privacy. This was done at 9.30 a.m.

At 6 p.m. I dared a further peep for, although I hate worrying mothers with new-born young, we have learnt over the years that things often go wrong in birth dens and one has to try to keep some sort of check going to decide the moment to move in and bottle-rear if necessary. I could only see two kittens but dare not look too much for the third. At 11 p.m. I looked again. Again two kittens. I was fairly sure a third lay dead somewhere but I will never know. A body was never found. We had by that time decided that if another kitten vanished, we would take the last one. Thank God this was never necessary. It is perfectly likely that there were only two anyway and the third kitten need never have been there at all.

Mother wildcat never looked back. Wayre had by this time made a statement in the press that the male must be removed or he might kill the kittens. I telephoned Dr Leyhausen in Germany at once and he told me always to leave the male in. This suited me well, since I always leave males in at births if possible. In due course, as the kittens emerged and played in their pen, the male loved them and they seemed to love him.

Sadly Broken-leg's wife did not give birth yet, but, being a late-summer-born animal herself, perhaps she would breed at about a year old we hoped. In the event, she had two kittens at three years old. Why should the Wayre female, admittedly captive-born, with a European parent and a Scottish parent be any different from the other all-Scottish female? There seems to be no answer.

The kittens grew well and played often. There was something about them, perhaps bigger feet, perhaps bigger heads, or both together, that gave them a special look, an undomestic kitten look. At exactly a month old they got out of their cage, squeezing through the two-inch chain link—something I would not have believed possible. We had to cover the whole cage with $1\frac{1}{2}$-inch netting, a disturbance for the mother I could have done without but, like everything else, she took it well. The day they got out they did in fact leave their own two-inch netting, then went through the two-inch netting of the buzzards who live next door. There, in their own little nest among thick nettles, they were found happily sleeping—

A distinctive Abyssinian, said to resemble closely the cats beloved by the Ancient Egyptians

A little Red longhair kitten still with baby blue eyes

incredible luck that the buzzards had not seen them. If they had done so I fear both would have been killed and eaten.

The Wayre female and her family live in a cage deliberately tucked away in a corner. It is not easy therefore to see what is going on and much of what must have been delightful antics was missed by us. At the end of the breeding season I had to rush off to Africa for an urgent film and when I came back the kittens had had their injections and were looking quite grown up. They were male and female and, dreadfully tempted though I was to keep them and set up another pair, this meant another cage and a lot more money. With two completely unrelated pairs—indeed four completely un-related animals—I decided reluctantly that we were well covered for the future and I was thus compelled to sell the kittens that had taken me ten years to produce. One went off, the female, to be paired with its uncle in Cumberland and the other went to Dart-moor. This was done in mid-November in the year of their birth. Since then the Wayre female has produced six kittens in 1973 and five more in 1974.

In January and February 1973, many male wildcat noises were heard at night from both cages and we hoped that both females would breed and, despite severe financial problems still, I think if we did ever get a male and female kitten from the all-Scottish pair we would keep them both. It would be nice to hand-rear some more kittens but I do not want to interfere too much and mother-reared kittens do much better. I do not think this will be too great a loss. Both pairs of adults here have now settled down nicely and the only advantage lost in not being able to handle them is that we cannot easily boost their injections when necessary. But we have gone for-ward over the years and now have a series of crush cages which, despite the horrid name, are in fact quick and efficient for injecting and the animal suffers nothing.

In 1974 after 12 years of wildcats in my life, the all-Scottish pair did breed, the first all-Scottish birth in this country and this was since 1884—discounting the council zoo birth that went wrong. The past 12 years were amply rewarded when this happened, although nothing will ever be quite the same as those first three kittens in 1962, who were quite, quite special and could so easily still be alive and breeding to this day. Although their untameness in the end was disappointing, even untame they were remarkable, for I have not seen a wildcat since with their coats, colour or, most im-portant, their tails. Perhaps they were 100 per cent pure; perhaps

G

Despite my condemnation of the inaccurate rumours which must circulate in smoky Scottish pubs about the fiercest animal alive, the totally untameable wildcat, who knows, could it be that that is why my special ones 12 years ago did not breed until they were four years old? We may never know. But although I can still hear the incredible banging of those three sets of heavy kitten feet as they romped around the room with my Alsatian, although the memory of the loving gestures of full-grown wildcats on my shoulders is still crystal clear and, although I can perhaps say I and I alone have tamed the Scottish wildcat, it didn't last very long did it? If taming means tame for life, then that bundle of wild-eyed fury from the distant and only unspoiled area of the British Isles *is* untameable and I have a deep-rooted feeling that I want it always to remain so. Of the hundreds of animals I have known in the past 20 years, I can think of none I would less like to see in a gin trap than the noble wildcat—*please Scotland, change your laws*. No one in this world can justify such unspeakable cruelty in an age when man is on the moon, even if a few less grouse are maimed by the waiting guns as a result.

Cat's ear has a long history in Europe where it is allied to and resembles the hawkweed, but with its hairy basal leaves shaped like those of the dandelion. The name is also applied to some hawkweeds in this country and to other plants with leaves suggestive of a cat's ear. In medicine cat's ear is a malformation of the human ear causing it to look like that of a cat.

GILEAN DOUGLAS, *Cats in our language*

4
Caring for your Cat

No cats about the house

COMPTON MACKENZIE

After the death of Edward I decided against having another Siamese cat at Denchworth. I did not believe that Denchworth would be our final abode and was only waiting until I could find the right surroundings in Scotland for books and cats before I left it. When that happened it would be time to have a cat again. Nellie Boyte had a large neuter tabby called Poodge; he was a wise and dignified animal and his death was a great grief to all.

I take this opportunity to preach a little sermon. If anybody makes up his mind to own a Siamese cat he must make up his mind at the same time to be owned by the cat. There is no point in having a Siamese cat unless one is prepared in the eyes of the world to spoil it. Unfortunately too many people nowadays acquire a Siamese cat because so many other people do. Such people are not qualified to be entrusted with a Siamese cat. For my part I strongly object to people who keep an old-fashioned tabby as a kitchen appendage.

However, this tiresome habit is so engrained that it is a waste of eloquence and emotion to try to cure people of it. The damnable folk who go away for their summer holidays and leave their cat behind in some respectable suburb think that if they ask a neighbour to put some food and milk in the potting shed for the animal they have left behind they have done all that can be expected of them.

'Cats are always much fonder of a place than they are of the people in it,' they will say with that fatuous complacency of the stereotyped mind.

Sometimes the neighbour feeds the cat; sometimes it does not. Cats are not scavengers like dogs, and to drive a cat into scavenging is a sin against nature. I am strongly in favour of making a cat's licence compulsory like a dog's. Yet for reasons I am unable to follow the Cat Fancy as a whole have always opposed a licence for cats.

Siamese cats are not left behind when their owners go away for the summer holidays. Why? Because people have usually had to pay for the pleasure of feeling fashionable in the ownership of a Siamese cat and so it is provided for in absence. I maintain that to charge cat owners even the inadequate 7s. 6d. that a dog licence costs would make them better aware of their responsibility.

However, although people with Siamese cats do not disgracefully abandon them to suit their own convenience, far too many of them are quite unworthy of the privilege of keeping a Siamese cat. They do not realise that Siamese cats must be 'spoilt' if their owners wish to get the best out of them, or indeed anything at all out of them. Nobody who understands and loves Siamese will disagree with that statement. If you meet a dull Siamese in a household you may be sure that the people are dull in the opinion of their cat. Dogs and Siamese cats get on together well if the dog accepts the fact of the cat's superior status in the household, and this an intelligent dog will always do. But if the members of the household pay an exaggerated attention to the dog the cat will despise them for it and will often desert that household as unworthy of its patronage. I have known several instances of this.

'Cats are so selfish. Cats think only of their own comfort. Cats have no loyalty. Cats have no affection . . .' and so on and so on.

Let it be granted at once that the dog will pander to its master's weaknesses by a demonstrative display of its dependence upon that master, but let it also be granted that the love of a dog is immensely much easier to win than the love of a cat. The personal relationship between Siamese cats and the man or woman who understands them often tempts the visitor to observe that Siamese cats are more like dogs under the impression that he is paying his host's cat a great compliment. Those who acquire Siamese cats because they think they will behave like dogs are in for a disappointment. A dog is never demanding: it responds to the demands of its master. Siamese cats are the most demanding animals in the world, and unless you are prepared to surrender to those demands it will be wiser not to keep a Siamese cat. I have seen many performing cats in circus shows but I have never seen Siamese cats perform and I question the ability of anybody to train them to perform. Lion-taming would be an easy job compared with that.

I regret that I have never enjoyed an intimate friendship with one of the large cats. I envy those who have been on familiar terms with a lion or a leopard. I met a cheetah once, and I have never been more gratified than when this great lovely cat rolled over and purred when I scratched it under the chin. A friend of mine in Burma once had a leopardess who slept at the foot of his bed for over two years. Then one day when he was being attentive to the little daughter of a high official he noticed a look in Ruth's eyes (Ruth was the name of the leopardess) which made him think she was about to spring. He caught her quickly by the collar, but he felt he could not risk having her loose about the house any more, and so he presented her to the Rangoon Zoo. He used to visit her every day but she pined for him too much when he was away and a fortnight later she died of grief.

I think one would probably have to be a bachelor to win the devotion of a great cat. Siamese cats are intensely jealous, but their jealousy is manageable. A jealous lioness or leopardess would be another matter.

I have read several accounts of lion cubs growing up as domestic pets but I fancy that they always have to be banished soon after they are full grown.* My friend's leopardess is the first I have heard of as a friend of man. Lion-taming and tiger-taming disgust me because I believe the relationship is based on fear, not upon affection, and if I had my way I would make performing tigers and lions illegal entertainment.

* When I wrote those words the story of Elsa the lioness had not been published. *Born Free* by Joy Adamson has been a revelation. To Elsa I have dedicated *Cats' Company*.

I have been told that the puma makes friends easily with man but I have never heard that the other great South American cat, the jaguar, was capable of domestic behaviour. Our own wildcat in Scotland can never be tamed. The kittens will spit and growl at a human being as soon as their eyes are open. And the offspring of a union between a wildcat and a domestic cat that has run wild are equally savage. I have only once seen a genuine wildcat in Scotland and that was in Glen Affric in the days before hydro-electric development. It crossed the road in front of the car and went bounding up the brae on the other side, turning round about twenty yards up to curse us. I was telling this story to my companion in a jeep when driving through the jungle from Kalewa to Pyangaing in Burma and saying I did not suppose I should have the luck to see a leopard, and as I finished speaking a leopardess with her cub crossed the road and plunged up the slope of the jungle. This is an unusual sight in the daytime.

That's enough about the great cats. I have no more chance of keeping one in Edinburgh than I should have of keeping a giraffe, which is an animal to which I have been greatly attracted ever since one leant over its railings at the Zoo nearly seventy years ago and pulled some of the flowers out of the hat our strict governess was wearing.

During the years I was without the company of cats I was never for a moment tempted to get a dog. There have been only two dogs in my life to which I have been deeply attached. These were the bulldog Smut whom I mentioned earlier and an Old English sheepdog called Bob whom we had in Burford and Cornwall and who came to live with my publisher Martin Secker at Iver when we went to Italy. I recognise the gratification and encouragement that a dog can be to countless men and women but I should derive no comfort from a dog's assurance that I was a wonderful chap. I should regard such an assurance as too easily earned. No man may be a hero to his valet but every man is a hero to his dog. The dog is a romantic; the cat is a realist. That will serve as a rough dichotomy, but it should be added that spaniels are sentimentalists.

The Pekinese and the Chow have as much realism in them as cats. It is significant that the remarkable growth in popular esteem of the cat during the last thirty years has coincided with a decline in humbug. During the Victorian age when Papa's whiskers were the top nobody would have ventured to call somebody or something the cat's whiskers. I cannot trace the phrase beyond 1927 as an expression of praise. One of the tributes to cats I most dislike is to hear them called mysterious. I dislike the word equally as an epithet for women. The behaviour of women is much more surely predictable than the behaviour of men. The only mystery about the cat is to know why it ever decided to become a domestic animal. The most plausible explanation is that the cat once upon a time discovered that man was able to provide it with that comfort which the cat regards as the object of its existence. I detect a parallel to be drawn between the cat's attitude and that of the woman who for the sake of security will tolerate existence with a man whom the rest of his sex regard as intolerable.

The anti-cat party cites this desire for comfort as evidence of the cat's selfishness, but no cat I have known has ever claimed to be an altruist. When it surrenders to love an individual man or woman it is always a possessive love and jealousy is dominant, all the more dominant because it is generally indifferent to human attentions and unprepared to acknowledge them. Dogs are jealous but it is a competitive tail-wagging jealousy without depth of feeling, the sort of jealousy children display when showing off. Of course, there are innumerable exceptions. I have mentioned that Skye terrier whom my mother gave to her sister when she married and who would never speak to her again.

For me one of the pleasures of cats' company is their devotion to bodily comfort. To look up from the sheet of foolscap on which I am struggling to find the right words in the right order and see on the other side of the room a huddle of cats asleep in perfect tranquillity is as restful to my mind as the cushion on which they are lying is restful to their bodies. I feel that to avoid disturbing them I must stick to my work.

Then there is the independence of the cat which is so absurdly resented by the dog lover. I welcome such independence. Mind you, it can be carried much too far by some cats, though I suspect that when it is carried too far the people of the house are to blame because they have failed to convince their cat that they regard it as a friend and not as a mere appendage of the household. Siamese are dependent on human company and they are never contented indoors unless they are in human company. For that matter they are always happier out of doors if people are with them.

If the friends go away for a time no cats, not even Siamese cats, will welcome their return with the faintest effusion. They seem anxious to impress upon the prodigal who has returned that his absence had been unnoticed. The coolness of this reception will last until the regular routine of the household's existence is resumed. Then without any marked demonstration of pleasure the cat will fall in with that routine and merely by doing so convince you as it thinks that it welcomes your return. On the other hand, the dog will greet the returned prodigal with a boisterous display of pleasure. This naturally flatters the prodigal, and the dog's affection for him makes him believe that the dog is more faithful than the cat, and that the welcome he has received proves that the dog is the superior animal. We catlovers cannot argue the point, for if we do we shall be seeming superior by suggesting that we are able to get on without the outward and visible signs of love.

Dog lovers may rightly claim that nobody has a horror of dogs comparable to the horror of cats which affects some people. Anti-dog feeling never reaches further than cold dislike, but horror is not too strong a word for the feeling that cats can excite. How does one account for a man like Lord Roberts shivering with apprehension if a cat was in the room he entered? Was he carried off by a man-eating tiger in a previous incarnation? Was he overlaid by a cat in his cradle? The latter is a favourable explanation for a state of mind frequent enough in maturity. I do not find it a satisfactory explan-ation. I should have thought that if a baby woke up to find a cat sitting on its head it would be more liable to claustrophobia when grown up than to shuddering at the idea of a cat being in the room.

The strange thing is that if a cat senses antipathy in a person it will deliberately as often as not jump into that person's lap and ignore those present who would be only too flattered if it would jump upon one of their laps. The contrariness of cats is familiar to all who love them, and we discern in such contrariness the cat assert-ing its individualism and abhorrence of the herd spirit so increas-ingly noticeable in human beings. It would be in keeping with a cat's character deliberately to choose for its attentions somebody who found them unwelcome. How does the cat pick out in a room-ful of people the one person who least wants to be picked out? I leave the question unanswered.

Presumably it was the cat's individualism which led to the notion that it was a spiteful animal. It is significant, however, that it was not until the eighties of the last century that 'catty' came into com-mon usage for the veiled malice of feminine comment. The dog was still the noblest animal, at any rate in Britain. It would have been unthinkable then to talk about 'bitchy' behaviour as we do today because it would have cast a reflection upon a woman's morals rather than upon her manners. It is significant, too, that from the time when dog-worship began to decline a genteel euphemism like 'lady dog' became non-U. Let me add that I am not suggesting that people today are any less fond of dogs than they used to be in the Victorian age; it is merely that romanticism is out of fashion. There still exist hobbledehoy oafs who think it clever to set their dogs to chase cats in the back gardens of subtopia, but they are frowned upon by the great majority of their neighbours, and I observe among the children of today as much regard for the cat as for the dog. This was certainly not the case in my boyhood when excessive devotion to a cat was often regarded with suspicion as a sign of 'cissiness'. If Dick Whittington had turned again on Highgate Hill to become a Victorian lord mayor, he would have arrived back in London Town with a dog.

The stimulus I receive from the company of cats is their unflagging curiosity. The lesson is constant, and as I regard the preservation of curiosity as one of the great prophylactics against the dangerously sedative influence of old age I rejoice in the tonic example set by cats. Not a drawer can be pulled out but a cat must investigate its contents. It knows that it will probably find the usual collection of shirts or socks or handkerchiefs from which the wash has removed every interesting smell, but it will still investigate on the chance of discovering a novelty. Eldorado calls to it as long ago it called to Raleigh. Those who are considering the introduction of a Siamese cat to their house will do well to remember that Siamese are much more restless than Persian, half-Persian and ordinary cats. Siamese always have a perfectly clear idea of what they want whether it be a particular chair, a particular dish or a particular room. Therefore people who belong to Siamese cats must make up their minds to do a good deal of waiting upon them. Perhaps the characteristic of cats that many of their lovers find most attractive is their tranquillity. I fear that this tranquillity cannot be claimed for Siamese unless like children they are asleep. They compete with pot-holers and mountaineers in causing immense trouble to other people to extricate them from difficult situations. They are merciless to upholstery. They delight in making one get up from one's chair to let them into a room and then a few minutes later making one get up again to let them out of the room the arrangements of which have failed to suit the mood of the moment. I insist upon this aspect of the Siamese because few things depress me more

than the sight of a Siamese cat whose lot has been cast with people
unable to understand what it asks from life. Siamese cats are unable
to indulge in the self-pity which allays with gentle massage a chip
on the shoulder: they are just lonely and dull.

An old friend of mine once decided that he must have a Siamese
cat, but neither he nor his wife nor his children have the faintest
notion of how to treat a Siamese cat. I knew any advice from me to
them would be idle. So I offered it to the cat.

Self.　You're not happy here, are you?
Cat.　Oh, I'm happy enough. I'm well fed. I have plenty of com-
fortable chairs. The house was cold at first but since this business
they call central heating was put in I'm no longer chilly.
Self.　But you're bored.
Cat.　You've said it. I'm bored. Damnably bored.
Self.　Yes, I felt that.
Cat.　These people are perfectly kind. I've been living with them
now for nearly four years. But they are doggy people, and I think
they ought to have a dog.
Self.　Would you like that?
Cat.　No, I shouldn't but it would give me an excuse to leave
them if they brought a dog here.
Self.　Where would you go?
Cat.　There's a woman living about a mile from here whom I
visit occasionally. I think it would be a kindness to go and stay
with her because she is undoubtedly lonely. I can tell that by the
way she talks to me. I'm at my wits' end here for intelligent con-
version.

I took an early opportunity of asking my old friend why he did not
keep a dog. He told me that there was nothing he would like better
but that he was worried about the cat's reaction. A few weeks later
however, a golden Labrador puppy arrived, and my friend wrote to
tell me that the cat had left them next day and gone to live with an
old maid in the neighbourhood. The next time I went to stay with
my friend I called on the cat. I asked him if he was happy and was
glad to hear that he was.

'But do tell her not to waste milk on me and also to see that
there is plenty of water available.'

When I returned to Edinburgh I decided that it was high time we had a cat about the house again. The travail of the move from Berkshire was behind us and the presence of workmen was no longer liable to upset a cat. I was offered a Siamese blue-point kitten and in March 1954 Bluebell arrived in Drummond Place.

Cat's nose is the popular name for the stormy northwest wind of the Harz Mountains. Cat face is a blemish or knot in lumber. Cat skin is not only the pelt of a cat but, in English slang, a silk hat of poor quality. Cat's auricle is a condition in man where the auricle is doubled on itself and this may lead to cat's purr, a peculiar trilling sound peculiar to that and some other heart diseases.

GILEAN DOUGLAS, Cats in our language

The word tabby was derived from a kind of taffeta, or ribbed silk, which when calendered or what is now termed 'watered', is by that process covered with wavy lines. This stuff, in bygone times, was often called 'tabby', hence the cat with lines or markings on its fur was called a 'tabby' cat.

HARRISON WEIR, Our Cats and All about them, 1889

A vet's life

JOHN BOWER BVSC MRCVS

'Mrs Jones is on the telephone. Apparently her cat has just jumped off the sofa and its tail has dropped off!' My very able nurse had never delivered a more unusual or macabre message than that. At this stage I decided to speak to Mrs Jones myself as obviously there was some mistake—such a thing could not happen. It had! Mrs Jones's description of the furry object, about nine inches long, which was no longer part of Blackie the cat, left me in no doubt at all. I suggested she should bring both parts of Blackie in to my surgery where I hoped I could resolve the problem.

Blackie had indeed jumped off the sofa and lost his tail. About three weeks earlier, Blackie had been involved in a road accident from which he appeared to recover fairly rapidly. He had not regained the use of his tail, however, due to a 'stretch fracture' at the base of the tail. This type of fracture is caused by a car tyre trapping the tail while a cat is still crossing the road at speed. This had in this case led to the death of the tail but not of Blackie. A minor cosmetic operation was needed to tidy up what was left of Blackie's tail and Blackie was as good as new—certainly a few inches better off than a Manx cat.

Cats do have problems with their tails. They seem to pay dearly for the extra bit of balance that the tail may give them. I always think of tail injuries as happening in cats that nearly got away with it. The tail as I mentioned is a fairly common site for a road accident injury. It is also fairly often involved in injuries sustained in fights with other cats—presumably either in cowardly cats which were running away at the time (too slowly), or possibly in cases in which the aggressor unfairly pounced from behind.

In the surgery, cats can be more difficult to handle and restrain than dogs. If a dog is a little fractious it is possible to muzzle it to prevent a bite and of course its claws are relatively harmless. A cat, however, can only be muzzled with extreme difficulty and usually distress is caused. The result is less co-operation than if it were not muzzled, and its claws can inflict most unpleasant wounds to the veterinary surgeon, the nurse or the owner. To reprimand a dog when necessary can help; in the case of cats it only makes the situation worse. Patience is the only real answer apart from a sedative when really necessary. Luckily for the profession, the attitude of the owner of an unco-operative cat is usually sympathetic to the veterinary surgeon. This varies from the mild 'Do be careful, he may bite and scratch you' to the blunt 'Don't trust him—he's a tiger.' This latter type of cat is usually brought in to the surgery trussed up in a small bag with perhaps his head protruding. One client of mine brings his cross-Siamese (very cross Siamese!) into the surgery from the waiting room by holding onto the scruff of the neck only. In this way the cat is brought in with all four legs and 18 claws rigidly extended, teeth bared and a continuous meaningful warning growl coming from its mouth. I was horrified the first time this happened and tried to explain to the client that there were better ways of carrying his cat. However, a short abortive attempt to demonstrate other ways with his cat convinced me otherwise! I now see this cat only at his home, where he is considerably better behaved.

Some cats are great believers in the saying that attack is the best method of defence. The minute they are placed on the consulting table they make a determined attempt to climb up the person examining them. This is a highly effective method of avoiding an examination. Equally effective is the raised attacking forepaw when a hand comes anywhere near them. But once the cat is restrained by the scruff of the neck gently on the table, then it is usually possible to carry out a thorough examination.

A separate waiting room for cats away from their canine cousins is a sound idea in a veterinary practice, although this is not always possible owing to shortage of space. Certainly cats are more relaxed in such surroundings than sandwiched between a great dane and a wolfhound. It is always much safer to bring a cat to a surgery in a cat basket or zipper bag than just to carry it or wrap it in a towel. This minimises any risk of escape which we all know can and does happen, and also ensures that the cat does not obtain such a close view of his neighbours in the waiting room.

I recall one escape with amusement now but great concern at the time that it happened. The surgery had finished and I was just contemplating a quiet evening when the door bell rang. At the time I lived above the surgery so there was no escape during off-duty hours. I answered the door and found a client holding her cat closely to her without even so much as a towel wrapped round it. The owner had misread the surgery hours and was presenting the cat for a routine check on a fractured leg which I had encased in a plaster cast the previous week. The poor cat took one look at me, realised immediately who I was and took off. The owner struggled to hold it but to no avail and within three seconds the cat had disappeared down the path limping at lightning pace. I say limping because a quick look at the owner revealed that she was still holding the plaster cast! This was the one part of the cat that she had grasped when he struggled, to try and prevent him from escaping, but the Houdini had pulled his leg out of it and bolted! The story has a happy ending which is why I can now look back on it with amusement. Houdini had limped straight home and was promptly returned to the surgery in a zipper bag. I applied a further plaster cast and within four weeks his leg was as good as new.

The most astonishing escapologist I ever handled was a ginger tom called Sandy. Sandy lived in a small coastal fishing village and true to form on a Saturday evening ate a piece of mackerel which unfortunately still contained the hook. This inevitably caught in Sandy's throat and my services were needed. This was no simple matter; the hook was anchored firmly in the throat and Sandy was in no way appreciative of my efforts to remove it. There was no

It can scratch too—house cat at play

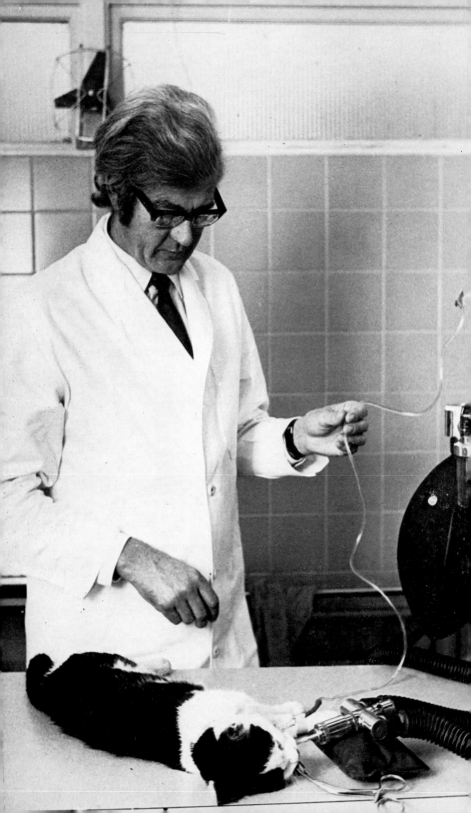

alternative but to take him back to the surgery for a general anaesthetic in order to remove the hook. Sandy was popped into a strong wicker basket and placed in the back of my estate car. The sliding windows of the estate were closed. After a few miles I decided to telephone the surgery to make sure there were no further urgent calls on the way back. Luckily there were not. On my arrival at the surgery, I lifted the basket out of the car and noticed that it was surprisingly light. Sandy had gone! The car, of course—he must be in the car! But I could feel myself beginning to panic. Mislaying a patient is not a common occurrence and I was hoping that this was a false alarm. It was not—Sandy was not in the car either. One sliding back window was now open. While I had stopped to make the telephone call, Sandy had escaped from an escape-proof basket (I have since decided that no wicker baskets are escape proof!), opened one of the sliding windows and absconded. All of this at least ten miles from his home, on the wrong side of a very wide estuary, and with a fish hook in his mouth. I think it was at this stage that I nearly joined the Ministry—and not the Ministry of Agriculture at that!

How was I to explain this to his devoted owners? I decided that there was no substitute for the truth, which I proceeded to tell them over the telephone. The news was received with unbelievable calm and equanimity, and apologies for not telling me that Sandy would open sliding doors, cupboards and windows. I assured them that I would alert all the other veterinary practices, RSPCA and police. This I proceeded to do but of course none of them at this stage could help.

Three weeks later the RSPCA inspector arrived out of the blue with Sandy (dear, lovable Sandy) whom he had just picked up on the other side of the estuary from that on which he had been lost. I cannot explain to this day whether Sandy is a strong swimmer or had in fact jumped out of the moving car nearer to my surgery than I originally thought. Anyway Sandy was back and looking fat and healthy at that, but with the fish hook still firmly embedded in the back of his mouth. He had obviously managed to eat well despite the presence of the hook. I rapidly administered a general anaesthetic and removed the hook. Sandy was then returned to his surprisingly grateful owners and I exchanged all my wicker cat baskets for fibre-glass ones.

I suppose this escapology is one aspect of intelligence in cats. It varies from cat to cat and my own three Siamese demonstrate quite clearly how the application of intelligence can vary. Guilia and Sadie are mother and daughter, and make up a very efficient door-opening team. They cannot open a door with a round knob but are experts at door handles. Sadie, being younger and fitter, jumps up at the handle and pulls it down with both forepaws as she falls to the ground, while Guilia, with precision timing, scrapes at the base of the door when the handle is depressed and opens it. They are so good at this that I have had to reverse the door handles of rooms which are forbidden to cats. The lounge falls into this category as the cats regard the lounge suite as their scratching posts. Rudyk, our third Siamese, has found an answer to this door provided we are in the lounge. He has noticed that when the front door bell rings, we open the lounge door to go to answer it, which is when he nips in. He has also noticed that in the bedroom upstairs is an old-fashioned tassel pull to a bell which used to summon the maid in some past era, and that both bells sound alike. Amazingly he has put two and two together and when he wishes to come into the lounge, he runs upstairs, pulls the tassel, waits until one of us opens the lounge door to answer the front door and into the lounge he goes. We had not the heart to disconnect this bell.

Some of the more amusing incidents in the course of a working day are concerned with the sex of the cat and the problems arising if the owner is wrong about it. I see male cats called Sue and females called Jason but luckily a substantial proportion of Fluffys and Blackies, names which could apply to either sex. Owners can become quite indignant if told that the cat is not in fact the sex that they thought it was. I recall a huge obviously masculine tabby with the typical male development of the cheeks and wide head, being, presented at the surgery for the spay operation. I pointed out tactfully that spaying was the term applied to the female operation but that the male operation was called castration. To this the owner pointedly replied that she was aware of this and her cat was of course female. I rapidly checked that my original impression of the masculinity of the cat was biologically correct (which it was) and feeling quite relieved reassured the owner that the cat was indeed male. 'But it can't be,' replied the owner, 'it's called Tinkerbelle.'

The terms used for these routine operations are also great fun when modified by clients. Female cats are brought in to be splayed or sprayed; males to be incarcerated or castigated, while either sex can be brought in to the surgery to be neutralised or nurtured. One proud owner presented a superb little kitten and exclaimed 'I want to know whether it is a boy or a girl and if it is a girl I want it incarcerated.' She was obviously terribly confused!

These operations are perfectly routine and side effects are virtually nonexistent. In the case of dogs, bitches occasionally put on weight when spayed but only if fed too much of the wrong food. Cats, however, seem to regulate their body weight by correct feeding and exercise. Very few cats become highly overweight. An exception is a neuter male I am at present treating for a bladder complaint. He weighs 36 pounds. When one considers that ten pounds is a fairly healthy weight for a normal male, this one is obviously grossly overweight. He somewhat resembles a miniature seal and is so wide that when he sits lengthways along a wall, one front leg hangs down on each side of the wall. How he manages to climb the wall I have no idea! Apart from his present problem, which is not associated with his obesity, he remains active and healthy and loving with his owners. He does however resent my presence and interference for some reason and tries to make life difficult. Because of the amount of fat under his skin, he has no scruff, as this is obliterated by the fat. The scruff of the neck in cats was designed purely and simply for veterinary surgeons to hold onto while examining the cat and when it is nonexistent restraint of the cat becomes a major problem.

Some cats however appear to like and respect us. A colleague tells me of a blue-point Siamese cat called Buttons, brought to his surgery by his owners who in fact live only a few doors away. Buttons had an injury to one ear causing a large blood blister which had to be drained under an anaesthetic and then sutured to prevent its filling up again. The sutures are passed through the ear flap and knotted through a button to prevent the nylon suture pulling through the skin. Thereafter Buttons used to arrive on his own at the surgery about every third day to have his buttons checked and finally removed. The only time his owners came with him was the first time.

The life we lead is sometimes exhausting but invariably rewarding. It is very satisfying to see patients recovering: to see Ginger running and climbing again after having sustained a broken leg in a road accident; to see Suki and kittens thriving after a Caesarean operation; to see Sandy recover from the slug-bait poisoning or even feline influenza. We do get attached to our patients but as cats do not live to our life span, we necessarily see most of our patients pass on eventually over the years. It is very sad to see an old patient pass away when one can remember delivering him or her what seems like only yesterday. It is an interesting life, however, and the many bright moments brought about by such incidents as I have mentioned, either by the apparent wit of the cat or often the wit of the owner, send one home chuckling at the end of a hard day.

In September, 1850, the mistress of a public house in the Commercial Road, London, going late at night into the tap-room, found her Cat in a state of great excitement. It would not suffer itself to be stroked, but ran wildly, to and fro, between its mistress and the chimney-piece, mewing loudly. The landlady alarmed, summoned assistance, and presently a robber was discovered up the chimney.

Upon his trial it was proved that he had robbed several public houses, by remaining last in the tap-room, and concealing himself in a similar manner.

CHAS. H. ROSS, *The Book of Cats*, 1868

Nothing is so beneficial to a cat's health as change of air, and fanciers would do well to try and take one or two of their pets with them to the country or seaside. This is especially necessary if you reside in or near any large town.

FRANCES SIMPSON, *Cats for Pleasure and Profit*, 1911

Feline lodgers

MIKE SAYER

I frequently wonder how my wife and I ever became involved in the mind-bending game of cat-boarding but, looking back, the whole thing seems to have evolved quite naturally from breeding occasional litters of Siamese kittens and having some of them back to stay during their new owners' holidays.

In our South London home, the occasional kitten or young adult would arrive to be a temporary house guest with our three queens and we found it extremely disconcerting to find its once loving and attentive mother turned into a snarling, hissing, fluffed-out monster who just would not tolerate the intruder. Often the hapless visitor had to be confined to a bedroom, complete with toilet tray and toys and once, when several cats turned up in the same fortnight, even the bathroom was pressed into service, causing havoc as one member of the family after another attempted ablutions before rushing off to school or office. The contortions necessary to squeeze through

the doorway without letting the 'inmate' esape were a sight to be-
hold.

Eventually it became apparent that we had to put the whole pro-
ceeding on a more business-like basis, with a set charge for boarding
and some proper accommodation built to adjoin the existing stud
quarters in the back garden. This decision was reached after three
weeks of trauma, when Sooty came to stay. Sooty was the pet name
of a seal-pointed Siamese male of our breeding, bought by very
good friends of ours who owned a printing works. He was a much
travelled cat, accompanying his owners to and from work each day
and to Wales for the weekends. He was rather spoiled, we were
told, and loved to roll on the cool enamel of the bath-tub, or to
drape himself on the stairs of the printing works. When his owners
decided to holiday abroad, Sooty came to stay with us and soon
settled in as one of the family. All seemed well and we looked forward to a straightforward three weeks with no problems on the
horizon. However, the first Sootyism happened at 7 p.m. that very
night.

My wife, about to bath my two small daughters, had run the hot
water into the tub and added the foam with which they loved to
play. She was undressing them when a mild tornado fled up the
staircase and sprang straight into the suds. Sooty, after the initial
shock, surfaced, exploded from the foam, and went into orbit around
the entire house, shedding froth wherever he went, until eventually
we were able to catch him, now looking like a shorn lamb, and to
rinse and dry him off. After that incident he took to jumping onto
the rim of the bath before getting in for his roll and would growl
ferociously while he made his inspection.

Sooty's greatest delight was to wait for my wife to start down the
stairs with a pile of laundry or some other burden that impeded her
view of the treads. He would silently run up the stairs and stretch
out on one step just as her foot was about to descend on it. As her
foot touched his soft body and she lost her balance, grabbing at the
handrail to recover, his howls would fill the house and he would
move down a few steps waiting to repeat the trick, eyes squinting
and tail lightly swishing.

On the fourth afternoon of Sooty's stay we called him for his
meal but there was no response. We searched the house from attic
to basement but could not find him. We looked under the beds,
through the chests of drawers, behind the cooker and in the airing
cupboard, and called and called, until, sure that somehow he had

managed to get out of the house, we sank exhausted into kitchen chairs. As I leaned my weary head back against the wall, my raised eyes met two others, slightly squinting, sapphire-blue and unblinking. Sooty was stretched full length along the top of the open kitchen door, one black gloved paw nonchalantly swinging.

Day eight produced Sooty-the-chimney-sweep act and it was our own fault entirely, because we should have remembered that on the very first day in his new home as a 12-week-old kitten, Sooty had disappeared up the chimney, hence his rather non-Siamese pet name. Unfortunately this time he chose the fireplace in the lounge and the white vinyl couches and sheepskin rugs have never really been the same since.

The real crunch came after ten days when Sooty went on hunger strike. Convinced that it was just because he missed his doting owners, we decided to do as they did and let him sleep on the bed. First of all he settled comfortably on the bottom of the double bed and we all went off to sleep, only to be rudely awakened by heavy breathing on the pillow at 1 a.m., and again at 2 a.m. and so on at intervals until dawn broke. With the dawn chorus and the first rays of sunlight through the window, Sooty decided it was time for everyone to get up. He tore around the bedroom, without once touching the floor, and made occasional sorties onto the bed to grab at my feet through the bedclothes and to bite my toes—hard! It was impossible to move a muscle, for every movement resulted in an attack from the 12-pound cat and only when he tired of the game could my wife and I get up. That morning we went out and bought two aviaries with flights and, with a few minor adjustments, converted them into cat chalets and runs. That night Sooty was firmly placed in one of them and the door securely bolted.

Shortly after the Sooty saga, we moved to the Sussex countryside, increasing our own family of pets, and soon the two aviaries were in regular service, housing other folks' cats most of the time. It soon became apparent that there was a great need for a good boarding cattery in the area. A visit to a local garden centre introduced us to some rather well-designed duck houses, made of deal, and after a chat with the proprietor, he agreed to make some slightly modified versions, this time in cedar wood, which would form the nucleus of our proposed cattery. Lorry loads of timber, great churning trucks of cement and miles of wire mesh were delivered and later, with blistered palms and a black and much hammered thumb, I proudly surveyed a neat cattery unit of two facing rows of five chalets and runs with a safety zone between. Panicking at the amount spent on this project, we inserted a small advertisement in the local paper and were immediately swamped with bookings. The following year more chalets were added and later, in the paddock, a block of 20 smart brick kennels arose. Nine years have passed and my wife and one of my now teenage daughters run a happy, successful business.

A whole book could be written on the joys and pitfalls of cat-boarding, although in the main the problems that occur are not with the cats themselves but in our dealings with their owners. We do not board entire males unless they are registered studs, and then they have special accommodation. Entire toms have a most un-pleasant habit of spraying all over their temporary abode which is then rendered untenable for any other cat for the rest of the board-ing season, no matter how rigorously it is scrubbed and disinfected. Toms also have psychological problems as regards territorial rights, which can make them mean to handle when away from their own patch. When we try to convey these problems to would-be clients, they are often most hurt at our refusal and are amazed when we tell them that cats can be neutered at any age. Happily most do agree to have the operation carried out and bring the often battle-scarred warriors in for their annual holidays.

The general public have many and varied terms for the altering of cats, be it castration in the case of the male or spaying in the case of the female. Our booking forms taken from the 'funny file' include under the entry for *Sex* 'muted', 'sprayed', 'nurtured', 'castigated', and, in the case of one lovely foreign black, 'female spade'. The forms also include space for *Favourite Diet* and entries range from tripe, lights and giblets to Mediterranean prawns (a cat from SW3) and, in one case, *Spaghetti Bolognaise* for a cream colour-point known as Gobbley who, to our amazement, when presented with this dish, proceeded to suck in the spaghetti by the yard with great aplomb. Other cats have more conservative tastes liking 'anything so long as he sees it comes from your own plate' to 'early morning tea, with sugar'.

We usually ask owners to bring their cats in to the cattery in containers, as on several occasions a car has drawn into the yard, all four doors flung open by various members of the family, and the cat, by this time thoroughly upset by the journey and strange sur-roundings, has jumped out and disappeared into the blue. Despite calling and coaxing by the owners, the cat proves impossible to find and eventually they go off to start their holiday, hoping that we will be able to recover the stray animal. In these cases, the RSPCA is contacted for the loan of a metal cat trap and advertisements are placed in the local papers offering a reward for information leading to the capture of the lost cat. When the bewildered creature is finally located, sometimes after weeks at large in a strange area, the trap is set with tempting food and usually successfully sprung after a few nights. This procedure is all very time-consuming, frustratingly worrying and expensive, also very detrimental to the health and temperament of the cat, so we do try to impress on clients the necessity of a container of some sort. And some sorts we get!

Cats have arrived here in enormous laundry baskets, tuckboxes, bicycle saddlebags, handgrips, picnic baskets, carrier bags, pillowslips and, in one instance, entangled in a string vest! They also come in lovely cane baskets, plastic-covered mesh carriers and the very useful disposable cardboard-carton carriers obtainable from most veterinary surgeons. In the case of the latter, however, it is most important to follow the assembly instructions correctly. Felix, a 20-pound red tabby, arrived to board one day and the owner placed the carrier on the floor of the office while she filled in the booking form but, when it was lifted up to take into the cattery, the handles and top lifted clear off and Felix was left sitting with a bemused expression on the base, on the floor—the base had not been locked into position correctly and Felix's weight had pushed it through the bottom of the carrier.

Most cats board very well, settling down within two or three days, and, if provided with their favourite food, eating well. Even cats which spend most of their time out of doors usually adjust to confinement and it is very rare to find a cat that will not use a toilet tray. Occasionally, however, the neurotic puss is admitted who decides to pull out all his fur, or one who digs up the vinyl floor covering, flattening himself underneath it and hoping no one will notice he is there and that he can quietly fade away without any fuss. Some decide to use their beautiful beds as potties and sleep in the toilet bowl, while others, when presented with their favourite dish of raw mince, kick litter all over it, making rude covering-up gestures with their paws, then spill the water bowl, finally paddling around in the resultant disgusting pudding until their pathetic cries bring someone to clean up the whole mess and give a sympathetic talking to.

Some owners are very considerate and bring bags of toys, bedding and hot-water bottles for their loved pets, even if the temperature is in the 80s, while others bring absolutely nothing. Even an old and grubby sweater can comfort a bewildered cat away from his own home, especially if it is the first time he has been boarded. It is interesting to note that it is often the cat brought without belongings whose owner makes the most fuss about abandoning him to our care for a fortnight.

One Siamese seal-point has been coming to us for nine years now. He always brings a lovely doll's cot complete with sheets and blankets into which he is lovingly tucked each night. One year he was accompanied by his own personal pet tortoise and he has recently taken to sporting a large blue bow tie to match his brilliant eyes, which he will not have removed even at bedtime. Simon is deposited with the minimum of fuss, although he is obviously a truly loved pet.

Another regular favourite is Flaps—his owners are keen aeronauts with a private plane—a dapper black and white shorthair, who always brings his own tiny cane armchair. Timothy, who happens to be a black *female* has her own very large and well-cushioned wicker basket and an enormous knitted draught-excluder-type stuffed toy from which she will not be parted. Others bring monster spiders, rabbits' paws and ping-pong balls and a new visitor this year, a Burmese blue, would not drink his water from anything other than his personal one-pint beer mug!

Some owners are very business-like in their approach to the boarding of their pets, leaving clear instructions as regards diet and an emergency telephone number in case of illness or accident either to their cat or themselves. Others are very emotional and find parting a real trial, breaking down and crying all over their animals, which, although understandable, is not very complimentary to us. And nothing is worse than being presented with a very soggy and tear-stained Persian late on a Friday evening—the end of a very busy week.

Most cats are in good health when admitted but a few arrive complete with a family of little parasites—fleas, worms, ear-mites and the like. It is very difficult to point out to a proud owner that their pet is less than perfect but very important that they should see and understand that these parasites need treatment and are contagious. Such cats are treated before being admitted to their chalet and further treatment follows at prescribed intervals. It is a wonderful reward to us to see a cat that has been lethargic and depressed, probably for months, with the irritation of earmites, suddenly perk up and play like a kitten, joyful at the freedom from these pests. Flea-infested cats are bathed gently in a protein and anti-parasitic shampoo on admission and, when dried off, skitter about happily free of the hundreds of daily bites that they have endured. Occasionally a cat is presented that is obviously far from well and in many cases an inspection of the mouth reveals lots of tartar around the teeth. This is pointed out to the owner and arrangements are made for the mouth to receive veterinary attention forthwith. Sometimes longhaired cats arrive with hair so matted that they cannot walk properly due to the hair between the legs being joined. We always insist that such cats are clipped, doing this ourselves if the cat is affable, but, if not, the proceedings have to be carried out at the veterinary surgery under anaesthetic. One irate owner refused to pay his bill when he returned to find his 'doormat' now resembled a French poodle, having a clipped body and full hair on head, tail and legs. However he relented when he realised how much happier his cat felt without the great wads and lumps of fur on his body. By far the worst thing that can happen to a boarding cattery is for a cat which is incubating cat flu to be admitted unknowingly. In a cattery run by people with a good working knowledge of cats in general, the very first symptoms will be noticed in time, so that the sickening cat can be isolated in good time, appropriate measures taken to prevent cross infection, and veterinary treatment started. In indoor catteries, or those run without sufficient knowledge, the disease can spread rapidly through all the inmates and may be fatal without dedicated nursing care. The dreaded feline infectious enteritis is rare in catteries these days, as most insist on all boarders being currently vaccinated but against cat flu, which comes in more than 50 varieties, no effective vaccine has yet been manufactured.

Boarding cats is very hard work and requires health, strength and an even temperament. During the season the telephone rings itself silly and there are seemingly endless toilet bowls to fill, trays of food to prepare, hours of grooming and, most of all, the endless scrubbing of hands, chalets and runs. Charges must be worked out to enable adequate maintenance to be carried out annually and to allow for the supply of both varied and good-quality feeding stuffs and the provision of extra labour whenever required. There are good catteries, bad catteries and many in-between catteries and many people are swayed by the wrong standards in their choice of what they want for their cats. Outdoor catteries are the best from a health standpoint but must be draught and damp-proof—cat flu cannot spread around in good, clean, fresh air but thrives in a warm, stuffy environment. Runs must be paved or concreted as it is virtually impossible to sterilise grass or earth between the arrival of one boarder and another, so that cross infection is inevitable. The wired-in runs must be escape-proof and the whole set-up should look clean and tidy without having a strong cat smell. The proprietor should have a good knowledge of the needs of the cat and, most important, an understanding of their psychology, as the success or failure of working with cats is based on knowing just what makes them tick.

Basically cattery management consists of cat charring. More time is spent in clearing up and cleaning out than in anything else, although cats are generally fastidious in their habits. During our daily routine a trolley containing all the necessary paraphernalia is pushed along the central safety area between the rows of chalets and for cleaning up spillage we use toilet tissue. A recent visitor asked what the toilet roll was for and when told 'Oh, it's for the cats' she looked astounded and asked how we taught them to use it!

Hard work and long hours, trials and tribulations, endless meals and piles of potties—we often wonder why we do it but we all love cats and welcome the regular faces year after year. We also get quite a kick out of seeing the holiday-makers, looking bronzed and fit, collecting contented pets who have also benefited from the change in routine—happy, well groomed and in blooming health.

A French writer says, the three animals that waste most time over their toilet are cats, flies and women.

CHAS. H. ROSS, *The Book of Cats*, 1868

Cat in the house

CHRISTINE METCALF

When a cat joins the family it provides the finishing touch. Like dotting the 'i' or putting the salt in your egg, it is the final contribution to make a house a home. What greater symbol of domestic bliss is there than a cat curled asleep before the fire? No animal is so complex as the cat. It can offer many moods, characteristics and poses to keep interest unflagging and boredom away.

Before taking a pet of any kind there are many things to consider. The advantages and disadvantages must be weighed carefully because you are taking the responsibility for a living creature for the duration of its life. Animals should never be given to children unless there is an adult prepared to supervise its welfare. Children can so easily become absorbed in something else and overlook a mealtime and they often tire of a pet when it has lost its baby playfulness. Every year many cats and dogs are abandoned when their owners grow tired of them. A watchful eye should be kept on very young children for they can easily injure the fragile bones of a small kitten or puppy. These are some things to think about when there are children in the household.

The advantages in choosing a cat for a pet are many and varied. The cat is a fastidious creature and it easily house-trained. The diet must be balanced and feeding must be regular but it need not be costly. Cats do not need to be taken out for walks, they will take their own exercise, although they can be trained to walk on a lead if you so desire. They are capable and reliable, well used to managing their freedom sensibly. Let your cat out of the house and it is not going to rush hysterically into the road or transport itself around the district seeking to sport with others of its kind. It will go about its business with decorum, will enjoy its freedom without getting into too much mischief, and will usually remain within call. This does not mean necessarily that it will come when called for no creature is more perverse than the cat. Nothing gives it greater pleasure than to outwit you when you are trying to get it to come in before it is ready. Useless to stand on a chilly doorstep making mealtime noises because the cat always knows if these are genuine and you can almost see a huge grin on its face as it fools you yet again.

The cat has a tremendous sense of humour and this game of 'catch me if you can' is only one of its tricks. Pouncing on an unwary passer-by is a favourite pastime in our house, especially through the banisters on the staircase. My lovely tortoiseshell likes to play the piano and will walk up and down the keys any number of times to make the notes ring out. I know a cat who knocks at the door when she wants to come in. A Siamese belonging to a friend, can open the door of the refrigerator in order to get at the goodies inside. Cats are very intelligent and can work out behaviour patterns when they are to their own advantage—but try to teach a cat to do tricks to order, or to repeat any of its own familiar ones and you will be rewarded with a blank stare. I have never seen a cat performing in a circus, not a domestic cat, nor have I ever known a cat owner able to persuade the pet to display any of its personal tricks. Perhaps one of the reasons for this is that the cat has great dignity and does not care to be laughed at. While it is always ready to share a joke, it can become very offended when it is the subject of the joke. Contrariness is very much part of the nature of the cat and although psychiatrists working with animals are able to condition rats, monkeys, dogs and various other creatures to react in mazes and with bells and coloured discs, they cannot use cats in the normal tests for intelligence because there is no co-operation.

Cats can make very costly pets if you consider the value of ruined carpets, curtains and furniture but the responsibility for damage lies with the owner. It is necessary for the cat to keep its claws in first-class condition because these are its tools for clinging, when it is climbing, and for grasping—the cat is naturally a hunting animal and needs to grasp its prey. The action of clawing is to pull off the outer shells of the claws as they become worn; it also keeps the muscles and tendons which control the function of the claws, in good condition. Furniture can be protected by providing a scratching post or log for the purpose of clawing. If the kitten is shown at an early age that you would prefer it to use the equipment provided, distress all round can be avoided. The method is to hold the kitten's paws and put it through the motions of scratching on the post. In the early stages it will sometimes forget and return to the best armchair but if you are patient, firmly rebuking it and returning it to the post and going through the motions again, it will soon learn. On no account should you get angry or strike the kitten; you will only frighten and confuse it if you shout and its tiny, fragile bones could be very easily damaged by a blow.

House training is unlikely to present many problems, for the cat is naturally a clean animal. In the jungle the large cats need to cover their traces for the sake of safety. Your fireside tiger instinctively has the same habit. Tiny kittens, too small to be allowed the freedom of the outside world, must be provided with a tray filled with earth or a proprietary cat litter, ashes, peat-moss, or even torn-up newspaper can also be used. The contents of the tray must be changed frequently for the kitten will not use a smelly tray and it would be offensive in the house anyway. You must show the kitten the whereabouts of the tray and, if at first it is nervous and apprehensive in its new surroundings so that it doesn't make the tray in time, teach it what is required in the same way as with the scratching post, holding its paws and going through the movements of covering the earth.

Feeding need not be expensive or complicated but it must be regular. Tiny kittens need a small meal four or five times a day because the stomach at three months is no bigger than a walnut. As it grows the number of meals should be reduced while the amounts are increased. Two meals a day should be sufficient by the time the kitten is nine months old. A common error is to feed the cat too much fish. In fact the cat is a carnivore and meat is an essential part of the diet. Fish can be provided to vary the diet but too much can cause skin disorders. Another mistaken belief is that cats only drink milk: clean water should always be available. Take care to cut or mince food for kittens as they can easily choke on large pieces. Chicken and rabbit bones must be avoided because they splinter and can cause internal injury and all fish bones should be removed. If the kitten you buy is from a recognised breeder you will be given a diet sheet which should be followed closely. All cats should be given a balanced diet and a few drops of vitamin oil should be added to the meal in winter. Cleanliness is essential both for your comfort and for the health of the cat. All uneaten food should be removed immediately as, if left down, it can become stale or fly-infested.

Although cats are very fussy about keeping their coats clean and a familiar sight is the animal busily engaged completing its toilet, this should not be left entirely to the cat. Daily grooming is necessary to remove dust and loose hairs which would otherwise be swallowed and may cause furball in the stomach. Begin with a wide-toothed comb and follow with a finer comb, taking care to check for any mats or tangles that may be forming. After combing, a vigorous brushing is usually enjoyed by most cats and for a final touch, if you wish your pet to look especially beautiful, a rub with a chamois leather or a piece of silk will leave the coat glossy. The ear flaps and eye corners can be cleaned with dampened cotton wool. Under normal circumstances it is not necessary to bath a cat; it does not enjoy getting its fur wet. If it does need to be cleaned, a moist sponge followed by a rub down with a dry towel is adequate, or a dry shampoo or warm bran may be used but the powder must be brushed out thoroughly or it can clog the pores and cause irritation.

Do not be alarmed if you see your cat eating grass; this is a natural emetic. The cat will eat it in order to bring up any hair that has been swallowed. Should there be no garden available, grass should be grown in a pot so that there is a regular supply. If you are growing grass specially for your cat, cocksfoot is the variety it will like best.

Comic-strip writers depict the cat being put out at night along with the milk bottles. In reality cats should be called in at night. It is unkind to send it out of doors, especially when it is cold and wet, and even the mildest weather can change during the night. There

'I always knew you cared'

'I thought I saw a puddy-cat'. Longhaired Cream kittens in pensive mood

An inquisitive trio of Bicoloured kittens

are many reasons why the cat should be trained to stay home at night. A cat allowed to stay in is less likely to come to grief in the dark from passing traffic, neighbours will have less cause for complaint at caterwauling, and fewer birds would be eaten. Cats like to hunt, it is their natural instinct. The birds are most at risk at dawn when they are feeding.

Cat owners are more responsible than they used to be and for this reason there are fewer unwanted kittens about. More people are having their female kittens spayed and their male kittens neutered. This is good because it means there are fewer strays. If you are not planning to breed with your cat, whether it is a pedigree or a mongrel, it is advisable to have it altered. Left to its own devices, a female cat will produce several litters each year. She will give birth to so many kittens that it will become difficult to find homes for them and then comes the task of having those appealing scraps destroyed. In the past, unwanted kittens have often been drowned but this is a cruel practice. If it is ever necessary to have kittens destroyed it should be done at birth by a vet. By far the happier solution is to have the cat altered so that the cat population is kept within reasonable limits. It is preferable to have few well-cared-for cats than many left to fend for themselves; there is less risk of disease too.

In all cases of altering, the work must be done by a veterinary surgeon. The female is spayed by removing the ovaries and therefore a bigger operation is involved than when a tom is neutered. Usually this is performed at about four months but fully grown cats can be operated on with a minimum of risk. In fact, a cat that has already had kittens can still be safely altered. Both male and female cats are improved as household pets as a result of this operation. They are less likely to stray and are often more contented. An entire male, on attaining maturity, will wander all round the district calling on his lady friends, often returning home bearing the scars of battle. Those large alley cats with tattered ears are invariably unneutered toms. The unpleasant odour peculiar to tomcats also disappears when it is neutered. There is a difference of opinion about the most suitable age for this operation. In Britain the recommended age is about four months, whereas in the United States it is suggested that eight months is a good age for a male and after the first heat for the female. A vet will advise you and it is as well to consult one early so you can make plans in good time.

Personality differences occur in cats in the same way as in humans.

I

There are character traits which prevail in particular breeds, so before you purchase your kitten it is as well to find out something about it. For example, the Siamese is noisy and demanding, extremely intelligent, loves company and will easily make friends with other animals in the household. On the other hand the Burmese is extremely placid and calm—one of its special qualities is its gentleness. The Manx likes to play with children, to retrieve thrown objects and to be taken for a walk when trained to a lead. The requirements of your household will guide you to the most suitable breed.

When selecting a kitten from the whole litter do not choose the leader for he will not be so affectionate as the others. These are just general differences but when you get to know your own cat you will recognise its individual differences. One cat will be rather shy and retiring whilst another quite the reverse, brash and demanding. My own cat dislikes it intensely when we have visitors and makes herself scarce. When we are just the family she is completely changed, is a pest when I am knitting, gallops about the room playing a kind of 'pussy football' if I am trying to read, and in general makes her presence felt. Another cat I know loves the family receiving visitors and nothing pleases it more than to select the one who least likes cats to settle on.

It will take a little time for you and your cat to get to know each other well and also for you to learn the language, for language there is. Be patient for the new quarters will be strange, the kitten must have a settling-in period with no hustle, for it has left its comforting mother and its brothers and sisters who were always there for a romp. It is a traumatic time and you will, of course, talk to it gently to calm it and to let it know it is loved. This is when the understanding between you starts, the beginning of a beautiful friendship. There are many ways in which the cat can communicate with you. The way it holds its tail is significant; its purring tells you it is pleased; its chirrup of welcome when you return home leaves no room for doubt as to its meaning. These signs are common to most cats but there are other sounds and signs that go to make up your own cat's vocabulary and these you will learn from your pet. Many lonely people have formed a deep attachment to the cat because of this two-way communication.

The cat is almost as old as time and its history can be traced back through to prehistoric ages. It has played a part in religion, in Egyptian times, was almost a national asset in Roman times, and was feared and detested in the Middle Ages. Today the cat has settled down to an undramatic role in society but, nevertheless, people do not let the cat pass unnoticed. There are either cat-lovers or cat-haters—seldom do people have no feeling at all about them.

There is worldwide interest shown in enhancing the breeds and improving the strains. This can be seen in the cat clubs and societies to be found in many countries. There are shows held throughout the world to display the result of the care, attention and effort of the breeders of the finest specimens. Nor are the shows only open to those who breed pedigree cats. There are classes for pet cats, those who belong to no particular breed but who have the same kind of attention lavished on them. Shows are held usually in autumn and winter—information may be obtained from a local paper. You can add to the interest of owning a cat by joining a cat club. Not only will you meet people with similar interests, but ideas can be exchanged and advice obtained on many aspects of cat ownership also.

The cat is no paragon of virtue even though we cat-lovers tend to praise them loudly. It is not a betrayal to recognise its shortcomings for its virtues far outweigh these. Its perversity is amusing when you have the time to appreciate the joke but infuriating when you are in a hurry. It is a notorious thief, having no conception of ownership, and you must remember to put away the Sunday joint. Place against the annoyances, the elegant beauty of the cat, its humour and affection and there isn't much of a case to answer. Forewarned is forearmed, many of the difficulties can be avoided when you know the nature of your cat.

The City Commission at Deerfield Beach, Florida, has passed a law requiring cats to wear bells after complaints that the quiet moving felines were decimating the bird population.

Owners who fail to put bells on their cats can be fined £10.

Daily Express, 7 February 1974

Having kittens

ALISON ASHFORD

'If my mother knew about that she would have kittens.' How often a phrase like this is used to describe some rather shattering event and yet, why should we equate a happy cat-family happening with something disastrous? During the past 15 years I've been midwife and paw-holder to many cats in labour but nearly all my memories are happy ones.

Of all the many breeds of animals, the female cat must hold the record for being the champion at motherhood. Perhaps this is the reason why cat fanciers speak of female cats as 'queens'. Certainly no human queen could look as proud as does the feline queen with her new-born family purring contentedly between her paws. There is no doubt that she lies there *expecting* admiration. Unlike many animal mothers, she enjoys letting humans touch her offspring but as soon as they are returned to her she rapidly licks away every trace of human smell with a look of utmost disdain!

A human mother carries her unborn child for nine months. A feline queen carries her unborn kittens for nine weeks. Like her human counterpart the queen spends much of the final few days of pregnancy preparing the place for the birth. As with humans, everything must be spotlessly clean and the room must be warm. Unfortunately here the similarity ends, for the queen's idea of ideal surroundings for the kittens is usually the back of the airing cupboard amidst a pile of newly ironed undies, or even in her mistress's large hat-box, nestled close to the latest Mary Quant model.

Once the kittening place is chosen, a battle of will ensues between owner and cat and the battle is only won by the owner because the birth of the kittens is already in progress and the watchful owner may need to hold the little queen in the correct place until the newborn squeaks make her realise that she must forget her own selfish wishes and get on with the job.

The thoughtful owner will have prepared a large cardboard box filled with plenty of old newspapers. Even if the queen is intent on using the hat box she will usually condescend to tear up the newspapers to please the mistress. This paper is invaluable if the litter is a large one, as it soaks up any fluid and blood which is not cleaned up by the new mother.

Most textbooks on cats state that if a queen is in labour for a full hour without producing a kitten, a veterinary surgeon must be called as *something* must be wrong! My own vet had a very short sharp comment on this when I first quoted it to him and I have learned since that those authors must belong to the 'fear of having kittens' school of thought.

Fortunately the first litter of kittens that I saw being born were produced in a most perfect textbook fashion, all five kittens being born in an hour and 15 minutes and all afterbirths being dealt with by a very efficient new mother. Since then I have seen many variations on the birth of kittens but only once have I had to call on my vet. This was when the queen was getting on in years and just before producing the first kitten she decided it was all too much trouble and just went to sleep! This had me really worried but when I phoned my vet he calmly said, 'She is probably lazy—try walking her up and down the stairs.' It was 1 a.m., the house seemed dark and cold and helping a fat pregnant cat to walk up and down 14 stairs without falling is no laughing matter! After four trips it was obvious that I was on the losing side. I screwed up my courage and called the veterinary surgeon who kindly told me not to panic and to put the mother on a warm blanket in a basket and to bring her to his surgery. At 3 a.m. we staggered into the surgery where, after a quick examination, our vet said he would have to do a Caesarean section, as the queen had developed uterine inertia (the technical term for lazy tummy muscles). He must have sensed my panic as he told me there was no need to worry—it was a very simple operation nowadays. I was given a cup of hot tea to calm my nerves while my little queen was taken into the brilliant lights of the operating theatre. Less than 20 minutes later, my vet and his assistant came out smiling happily to show me a sleeping queen with a fairly small, neatly sewn seam and three tiny wriggling kittens who were already trying to sneak a drink.

A few hours later the little mother was purring contentedly whilst her kittens suckled and I stumbled around trying not to fall asleep over the housework. Needless to say, this little queen was spayed when the kittens were weaned, as she had earned her retirement. It would not have been kind to let her have another family, as she would probably again have had uterine inertia.

Although this has been my only emergency, no kittening day has ever been boring. One hears it said that cats like to hide away to have their kittens. This is only a half truth. It is true that a queen likes to find a dark quiet place in which to produce her kittens but she does *not* like to be alone. I have owned and been owned by 'moggy' cats, by Siamese cats and more recently by curly-coated Rex cats but always, when the labour-pangs start, I am needed to be close at hand. All my cat-loving friends confirm this and it seems a pity that the general public doesn't yet realise this fact.

Many people who decide to let their queen have a litter seem to have a fear of breach births. I shared this fear but the first two kittens that I saw being born could not have been more normal. The third one however was different. The little queen had been in labour for two hours when I saw a tail and a leg beginning to appear. I rushed to my textbook which of course said to 'Call the veterinary surgeon'. Unfortunately my vet knew I was a trained nurse and I suspected he might come back with a sarcastic retort. So I returned to the queen, rubbed her tummy and talked quietly to her and her purring recommenced until another desperate contraction caused her to cry out. I continued to rub her tummy for three more contractions but, though slightly more of the kitten's body appeared, the other hind leg was obviously caught up inside the vaginal tract. Something *had* to be done and I decided that I was the one who had to act. After scrubbing my hands till they tingled I dried them on a clean towel, then rubbed soap onto my little finger. Whilst my young daughter restrained the queen, I very gently inserted my soapy finger on the side of the kitten where the hind leg was still imprisoned. I could feel the little leg and, as I carefully pushed the leg towards the kitten's body, the queen gave a terrific push and a perfectly normal little kitten uttered its first plaintive cries as the mother licked away the sac. Three other kittens were born after this one and two of these were also breach births but by then the vaginal opening was well dilated and no further problems occurred.

For all parents who have reservations as to the best way of explaining the 'facts of life' to their children, a cat having kittens is the perfect answer. Ideally the children should have watched a young queen grow to maturity, seen her experience her first 'calls' and then they should see her taken to stud for her 'honeymoon'. A female Siamese in full call, making amorous overtures to the nearest living creature leaves nothing to the imagination! However, if neighbours tend to be critical of unusual noises, a quieter cat might be a better choice.

After the queen is mated, children can be encouraged to keep a diary of her progress through pregnancy, until the great day eventually arrives and the children can be shown how to be quiet and attentive midwives. My own two daughters, having assisted at several births, were adept at cutting kittens' cords with sterilised scissors, if the queen happened to prefer to wash the new-born kitten rather than to sever the cord and eat the afterbirth.

Those parents who believe in a puritanical upbringing for their children may find it difficult to explain away the fact that a queen will happily mate with a variety of tomcats. Even a queen with an impeccable pedigree will accept several alley toms if she has the opportunity! In fact, if the family atmosphere is happy most children will accept the fact that 'cats have not yet learned how to behave like human beings'. If the parents belong to a wife-swapping society, doubtless the children will decide that pussy has learned to behave like human beings!

More than any other animal, a cat likes to be spotlessly clean and a mother cat will push her kittens into a shallow sanitary tray as soon as they begin to walk. Young kittens obviously feel a sense of achievement the first time they scrabble a hole and use it for the correct purpose. They hate any human being to laugh at the serious expressions on their faces as they squat on the tray. An owner who forgets to put down a sanitary tray for young kittens has asked for trouble, as once a kitten has used a certain place to urinate, it will return to that place by its sense of smell and this habit is very difficult to break.

I have a hair-raising memory of the year we decided to let our poodle have a family at the same time as our Siamese was having kittens. By the age of 3½ weeks, the kittens were climbing into their sanitary tray. Not so the three puppies who, at the age of four weeks, were making large puddles all over the dining-room floor. Of course, they were twice as heavy as the fine-boned Siamese kittens. After witnessing several episodes when tank-like puppies had dragged kittens off their sanitary tray and through large puddles of urine, we decided that the puppies and kittens must live a separate life. In spite of my daughters' protests this was the one and only litter of puppies that we bred! It is a known fact that cats are psychologically soothing to those who are depressed or worried. But untrained puppies, I am sure, can be guaranteed to induce a nervous breakdown!

Sometimes a queen may take herself off for a night on the tiles without her owner's knowledge. With a maiden queen it is even possible for her to produce her litter to the complete astonishment of her owner. If this should happen and it is impossible to keep all the kittens all vets will put the unwanted kittens to sleep with an anaesthetic for a very small fee. It is always kindest to leave the new mother with one kitten otherwise she will be heavy with unwanted milk. No kitten should *ever* be drowned. As a young child, I was nearly drowned under a huge wave in East London, South Africa, and the memory of the terror of that moment is still with me. Drowning is a slow and cruel death, contrary to what many farmers will say.

Occasionally in a large litter of kittens one may be born that is a weakling or, as breeders say, a runt. It is quite easy to pick out a runt within a day or two of the birth as it will not increase in size as the normal kittens do and it often drags itself restlessly round the box, unable to suck for long on its mother's nipple. The instinctive reaction is to try to save its life. I have several times attempted to do this, hand-feeding the kitten hourly with a dropper and sweetened Carnation milk. But, whereas it is possible to feed a normal healthy orphan kitten in this way, it is only prolonging the runt's miserable existence. It will invariably die and the exhausting struggle has been in vain. So, if an owner finds a 'poor-doer' in an otherwise normal litter, it is kindest to have the poor little creature put to sleep before human owner and feline mother have suffered too much.

However, on the very rare occasion when kittens are, for some reason orphaned, it is quite possible to hand-rear them, using either a good-quality artist's paintbrush or an eye-dropper, or a special kitten feeding-bottle. Carnation milk mixed with one part boiling water to three parts of milk and half a teaspoonful of glucose is an ideal mixture to use. But tiny kittens need to be fed every two hours night and day and, following each feed, they need to have their tummies rubbed with warm cotton wool until they pass water and faeces. This rubbing action is a substitute for the rough licking of the mother's tongue and without it kittens will soon develop enteritis and die. It is a tremendous achievement to hand-rear a litter of kittens—but it is also a tremendous strain on the entire human family.

Although kittens do not normally start their weaning programme until they are over a month old, it is best for all concerned to start to wean orphan kittens at the age of three weeks. The two-hourly milk feeds should be maintained until the kittens are two weeks old, after which time three-hourly feeds during the day and just two feeds during the night are necessary.

A young kitten's greatest difficulty is to learn to stand and to lean its head forward to eat from a dish. Life can be made easier for owner and for kittens if the first semi-solid feeds are offered in a dessertspoon held up to the kittens' mouths as they stand upright. As they realise that there is something tasty in the spoon, they can gradually be urged to lean forward to a dish. Even the most difficult orphaned kitten can usually be persuaded to eat fine whitefish, mashed with a little milk. Hardboiled eggs mashed with a little Marmite are also accepted. Milk feeds should be changed to feeds of Farlene, made with Carnation milk and water. Finally at about four weeks of age, orphaned kittens will usually take readily to finely scraped raw beef.

By the time that orphaned kittens are ready to be vaccinated against feline infectious enteritis (and it is very important that all cats and kittens are vaccinated against this killer disease) the human family is usually living on bread and milk with an over-sized overdraft at the bank!

In spite of these drawbacks, orphaned kittens seem to demand—and give—an abundance of affection. Since they have never known a feline mother, there is little doubt that they regard the owner who has fed them as their real mother. Having reared a litter of four Siamese in this way, I found their resulting affection almost embarrassing. If I went to the lavatory there were angry howls until I opened the door and when I took a bath I was dive-dombed by nosy little kittens trying to find the quickest route from one side of the bath to the other. During this 'kitten period' I had to have a chest X-ray at the hospital where I work. I was rather surprised by the solicitous questions asked by the kind radiographer. It was only later, as I dressed in front of the mirror, that I realised he must have thought the long scratches on my back were the result of some kind of beating!

With orphaned kittens it is especially important that the right kind of home is found for them. I always insist that would-be owners visit at our home. It is quite easy to pick out the real cat-lovers from those who just want a kitten as a passing fancy. This type of person doesn't want to pick a kitten up and cuddle it. He will just point at the kitten he wants and say 'I'll take that one'. If this situation arises I just say that I've decided to keep all the kittens after all and the would-be owner departs convinced that I am quite mad—which I probably am!

Perhaps a word of warning to the unwary might not be out of place here. It is terribly easy to 'collect' cats, keeping a favourite from one litter, the tiniest kitten from another litter and the most unusual coloured kitten from the next. In a comparatively short time there can be cats in every room, a decidedly 'catty' odour around the house and tension in the family. The cats' fascination in a situation like this can be fatal, as with increasing numbers of cats, the possibility of feline illness becomes much more likely, the furniture suffers, family cooking suffers and in a comparatively short time there is a very real chance of a broken marriage and delinquent children.

My veterinary surgeon made the statement that cats are not pack animals as dogs are and that to keep more than five adult cats in an ordinary house is therefore inviting problems, certainly for the cats' own health.

These are only a few points about the many fascinating aspects of 'having kittens' and different people will have different experiences. But of one thing there can be no doubt—the cat is surely the perfect mother and there can be few sights more beautiful than a mother cat licking her young kittens to the accompaniment of ecstatic purrs.

In China you find the catsclaw, a twining fabaceous vine bearing white flowers. Cat's foot is the ground ivy, but also can describe a short, high arch-toed foot. Catspaw can be different things to different people. To the botanist of Tasmania it is a plant of the amaranth family. To the sailor it means to fasten together by means of a catspaw hitch : a twisting hitch in the bight of a rope by which to attach a tackle. Most of us think of the word as describing a person used as the tool of another for doing discreditable work. This comes from the fable of the monkey, who fooled the cat into pulling chestnuts out of the fire for him.

GILEAN DOUGLAS, *Cats in our language*

Any one who has tried getting kittens to sit for their portraits knows how difficult it is to make the fidgety little creatures be quiet. Try holding up a looking-glass so that the kit can see its own reflection. This experiment often answers splendidly.

FRANCES SIMPSON, *Cats for Pleasure and Profit*, 1911

The fundamentals of social hygiene

MARGARET COOPER GAY

Cats keep themselves clean and they have clean habits. Mamma cats house-train their kittens while weaning them, and you can be practically certain that any kitten you buy or otherwise acquire after it has reached the ripe old age of six weeks knows the fundamentals of social hygiene. It knows that, like all cats the world around, it must dig deep, wide, and handsome to conceal this evidence of its presence from roving enemies, or it must hide the evidence in some other, more ingenious manner. If you and the cat see eye to eye in the matter of privacy, all's well. If not, you'll have to find out what the cat wants and provide same.

Ordinarily, housebreaking a cat is no trouble at all. If the new cat is half grown or older, you simply make it feel at home with you, feed it, let it out in the yard and watch until you're sure the cat knows what yards are for. Call it in, and dismiss hygienic considerations from your mind. Next time the cat wants out it will tell you.

A little kitten is better trained to a pan at first, even if there's a yard. You might not be around when it wants out (which is about 20 times a day when they're little), or it might forget where the door is. In either case the kitten is likely to make sanitary arrangements indoors that wouldn't coincide with your ideas.

The location of the kitten's pan is important; you can't expect a small kitten to travel great distances in search of a comfort station. Neither can you put the pan in a different place every day and expect the kitten to guess where you hid it. The pan must be kept in one place, even though it inconveniences you, until the kitten grows up enough to cope with the vagaries of human nature.

Any large, shallow pan that doesn't leak and can't rust will do. A cheap, enamelled dishpan is fine for cats. A kitten needs a shallower pan, so it can see over the edge; cats don't like to jump blindly into cat pans.

What to put in the cat's pan is debatable. Some people use sand, but sand gets tracked around the house, scratches the floor and cuts the rugs. Also, disposing of used cat-sand is a problem for people who live in apartments. Shredded paper doesn't get tracked around; on the other hand it is neither very absorbent nor easily disposed of. If you put flat paper in the cat's pan the cat will shred it. I have found sawdust more satisfactory than anything. Sawdust can be obtained at any lumber yard or from the butcher. Sawdust is exceedingly absorbent, and pine sawdust out-smells cat for at least twelve hours. If it is handled with care, sawdust will not stop up the drain, which is a great advantage. The sawdust particles that get tracked around the house won't scratch floors or cut rugs and are easily swept up.

If you know you're going to get a cat, have its pan ready when it arrives. If the cat comes unexpectedly, fix its pan first thing. Show it to the cat at once. Then, as soon as you've fed the cat, take it to the pan again. Keep it there until it uses the pan. Don't clean the pan until it has been used a second time. Whatever you do, don't clean the cat's pan with carbolic acid or any other coal tar derivative. Wash the pan twice a day with soap and water and a long-handled brush and it won't need any other cleaning.

A woman I know bought a full-grown cat and a proper cat pan. Then she scalded the pan with carbolic acid solution, laid in it a folded newspaper, and expected the cat to use it. Even the odour of carbolic will make a cat ill, so naturally the cat didn't use its pan. A day passed, two days, three days, and the cat did nothing at all. The fourth evening she came home to find that the cat had sprinkled on each of the 24 buttons that tufted her daybed, messed in the waste-basket and left by way of the fire escape.

If the cat won't use its pan there's a reason. The location of the pan may be so public as to offend the cat's sense of modesty. The cat may have been educated differently; cats that have lived with writers, for example, are usually trained to some other cover material than paper, lest they get disrespectful notions about manuscripts. I used to know a cat that had been found in a disreputable alley and would not use a cat pan. He used wastebaskets and the garbage can and once he used a guest's top hat. His distracted folks finally decided he'd learned his manners in an ash can. They got him an ash can and he used it.

Some cats think they know more about comfort stations than people do, and take a fancy to the bath tub or the shower or the fireplace. I suppose the bath tub and shower fanciers are civilised cats who appreciate modern conveniences and resent efforts to impose primitive sanitation on them. Anyhow, they're usually stubborn. You might try keeping the bathroom door closed, if you can remember to close it, and if you can find a place outside the bathroom for the cat's pan. An inch of water in the bath tub and an inch in the wash basin might drive the cat to use the toilet, and then you'd have something to brag about.

One of my friends who had a pet wildcat, a real bobcat, invented an improved cat pan that some other cats might like. This was a large white enamelled pan, into the bottom of which she fitted a broiler rack made of fairly close, heavy mesh. Over this she put two or three large paper towels, and when the pan had been used she simply dropped the paper towels down the toilet and rinsed the pan with warm water. She kept a film of water in the bottom of the pan, with a scattering of soap flakes on the surface. The pan never smelled and was awfully easy to keep clean. Eventually the wildcat learned to use the toilet.

The fireplace habit is hardest to cure. Cats that can go out may prefer the fireplace. You may break this up by putting some used ashes from the fireplace in the cat's pan just this once. Then scrub the fireplace with soap and water, dust it thoroughly with the powder that is supposed to keep cats off the furniture, barricade the fireplace, and cross your fingers. If you keep the fireplace barricaded long enough the cat will have to use its pan. Once it starts using its pan the fireplace is safe.

If a cat that has been house-trained suddenly ceases to be, and you haven't been hiding its pan or messing around with smelly disinfectants, the cat is probably sick.

If the cat suddenly begins sprinkling a little here and a little there it has sex on its mind. This problem, which has nothing to do with sanitation, is deliberate advertising in defiance of caution, roving enemies, or punishment.

Just before the earthquake at Messina, a merchant of that town noticed that his Cats were scratching at the door of his room, in a state of great excitement. He opened the door for them, and they flew downstairs and began to scratch more violently still at the street door. Filled with wonder, the master let them out and followed them through the town out of the gates, and into the fields beyond, but, even then, they seemed half mad with fright, and scratched and tore at the grass. Very shortly the first shock of the earthquake was felt, and many houses (the merchant's among them) came thundering in ruins to the ground.

CHAS. H. ROSS, The Book of Cats, 1868

A Red-point Colourpoint kitten with beautiful pale body colour and contrasting red points

A Self Chocolate longhair kitten, an excellent example of a man-made variety

5
Cats around the World

Cats in North America

BLANCHE V. and RAYMOND D. SMITH

Cats have a long history in North America. Although there is considerable evidence that the native American wildcats—particularly jaguars—played a major part in the folklore and religions of the pre-Columbian Americans, there is no indication that even the smaller species such as the jaguarundi and the ocelot were domesticated in the sense that we use the term. In recent years these two smaller cats have been imported into the United States in quantities of some hundreds per year but, although intensive efforts have been made to popularise them as pets, results have been minimal. Veterinarians and humanitarians generally have inveighed against this practice and with the increasing concern with the welfare of our animals in the wild, the importation of such cats is meeting with increasing disfavour.

The domestic cats we know today arrived with the earliest settlers—there was a cat on the original *Mayflower*—and spread by knap-sack, stage coach, covered wagon and by foot almost as rapidly as the Europeans who brought them. Today the cat's importance is not primarily that of a protector of rural fields and barns from mice, rats and other rodents but its economic and social value is higher than ever before.

There are some ten million cats still running half wild in rural areas and in urban warehouse districts but they are out-numbered two to one by the 25 million pet cats owned by some 12 million North American families. Making up most of this grand total of 35 million cats is the typical domestic—the descendant of the ship and the pet cats who have been coming to the continent over the centuries from origins in Europe, China, India and most of the countries of the world.

About two million Canadian and US cats, however, have purebred backgrounds. The first American breed descended from eighteenth-century longhairs brought to New England who bred with the native domestics to develop the breed now known as Maine Coon.

Early in the nineteenth century came the Manx, the tailless anomaly from the Isle of Man. Then in the late 1800s began the almost mass importation—principally from England—of Persian longhairs, Russian blues, Abyssinians, and Siamese. At the same time, though, angoras were being imported direct from Turkey, Persians from India and Iran and Siamese from Japan and direct from Thailand. It was on these breeds that the American Cat Fancy was founded.

Starting at the turn of the century with the Beresford Cat Club (named from England's Lady Marcus Beresford), interest in cats has grown to the point at which there are now 250 cat shows a year, nine cat-registering organisations and some 20,000 active cat breeders entering more than 50,000 cats a year in these 250 shows.

Oldest of the cat registries is the American Cat Association founded in 1901; largest is the Cat Fanciers' Association which branched off in 1906 and now sponsors more than half of the continent's cat shows. The Canadian Cat Association confines itself almost entirely to Canada. The Cat Fanciers' Federation concentrates most of its activity on the east coast. The American Cat Fanciers' Association, the second largest organisation, features a 'democratic' system of government in which the final voice is with the members rather than the clubs or the boards of directors as with most of the other associations. Crown Cat Fanciers' Federation also features member government and it initiated the policy of permitting *any* registered cats to appear in its shows—not just those registered in its own stud book as do most other associations. The United Cat Federation is centred in the state of California; the Independent Cat Federation is a very small group on the east coast; mostly in the Midwest is the National Cat Fanciers' Association.

For many years, members of these associations were tied together by the All-American Scoring System, instituted in 1946 by *CATS Magazine*—the Cat Fancy publication. Under this arrangement every eligible cat on the continent is scored on the basis of its wins in every cat show and sectional and the national awards are given for each cat of every breed, sex and colour. In 1967 the Cat Fanciers' Association withdrew from the All-Americans but effective with the 1974–5 season, they will again allow All-American scoring of their shows, once again opening up a limited avenue of communication among the entire Fancy. A loose organisation of some of the independent (non-CFA) organisations has functioned fitfully since 1968 and is now being revived.

Since the first Fancy schism in 1906, there has been hope that the various factions would forgive and forget and form one united organisation such as in Great Britain where the fancier and exhibitor could enjoy the luxury of registering his cat and cattery only once, of having only one set of show regulations to absorb and only one set of show standards to go by. But, although in these past 70 some years the Russians and the Germans, the Indians and the English, the Chinese and the Americans have adjusted most of their differences and all the nations of the world have been able to work together in the United Nations, the various American Cat Fancy principalities continue to rule in their own spheres, having little or no intercourse.

While it is the Cat Fancy which receives the most publicity, of far more importance in the social and financial structure are the ubiquitous pet domestic cats found in at least one American home out of every five. Their social value has long been recognised and only recently a leading American psychologist, Dr Boris M. Levinson, professor of psychology at Yeshiva University in New York City, has published a study on pets and their relationship to humans —*Pets and Human Development* (Thomas)—in which he discusses the importance of cats in helping to form strong family relationships in this age when many of the traditional family-forming structures are weakened or absent.

Perhaps the most famous recent American cat was Tom Kitten who lived in the White House as the pet of Caroline Kennedy when her father was president. Other famous members of the feline family have been Rhubarb, who starred in the movie of that name based on H. Allen Smith's popular novel of a cat who owned a baseball team. An early 1960 mystery movie, *That Darn Cat*, starred a cat called by the title name who worked for the FBI. It was based on a novel by the Gordon Gordons. The only individual cat of the United States ever to appear on a postage stamp was the pet of Charles A. Lindbergh who had planned to fly the cat with him to Europe on his record-breaking 1929 flight to Paris. When the time for take off came, the cat was left at home because of the rough weather but the Spanish post office either was ignorant of the last-minute change or ignored it and put the cat on the same stamp as Col. Lindbergh and his *Spirit of St Louis*. A typical anonymous cat is shown on the 1973 United States postage stamp celebrating 100 years of American mail order.

About 20 to 25 books about cats, or with cats as central characters, are published in North America each year. Grace Pond's recent *Complete Cat Encyclopedia,* whose American editors were Blanche V. and Raymond D. Smith, was published in an American edition in 1972 and has enjoyed widespread success. It is by far the most wide-ranging and lavishly produced book on the Cat Fancy ever published here. The most scholarly and interesting study on cats as a whole throughout history, culture and art is Carl Van Vechten's 1920 masterpiece *The Tiger in the House.* That it is still in print 54 years later is a tribute to its quality and appeal. Claire Necker, an American librarian and bibliographist, has recently published *Four Centuries of Cat Books.* It is unique in that it contains a bibliography of every cat book ever published in English over the past 400 years —some 2,400 of them—by author and title with pertinent information on those of more than passing importance.

Since its beginning, the North American Cat Fancy has spawned 20 cat magazines of which records endure. Today only *CATS Magazine,* founded in 1945, and *Cat Fancy,* founded in 1965, remain. Both are professionally produced publications circulated throughout the United States and Canada and with small numbers of subscribers in most countries of the world. *CATS*, for example, goes to some 50 overseas countries. England, Australia and New Zealand take the largest number but Japan is a close fourth and copies go even to such places as Russia, Thailand, Turkey and

Hong Kong. *Cat Fancy* features editorial matter of a general nature; *CATS Magazine* devotes more than half of its space to the professional and the semi-professional cat breeder, with about 40 per cent directed to the everyday pet owner.

As cats have grown in number and as the standard of living of humans has increased, so has that of the cat in North America. Sales of cat foods now total $600 million per year—only slightly less than sales of baby food. For flea collars alone, North Americans are said to have spent $50 million in 1972. Some 15,000 American veterinarians accept cats as patients. Their income from cat clients is estimated to be in excess of $100 million per year. Cat-pan-absorbent sales total another $100 million. These items, plus such products as cat playthings, scratching posts, carrying cases, and incidentals, bring the total impact of the cat on the North American economy to at least $1,000 million a year. Cat foods, as has been pointed out in recent Congressional hearings on the American diet, are more carefully supervised than are human foods. Each can lists the ingredients and the nutritional value—information which we humans have not yet earned.

The recent shift in American birth-rate trends does not foreshadow a similar decrease in the cat population. Instead, indications are that pet cats will probably show a 50 per cent increase in number by 1985 and cat expenditures will triple.

For the Cat Fancy, projections are even more optimistic. Whereas about 50,000 pure-bred cats are now being registered yearly, projections for 1985 are for at least a quarter of a million registrations. By that time, too, it is expected that there will be more than five million pure bred—but unregistered—cats and kittens, that cat-show entries will exceed 200,000 and that close to two million cat fans of the United States and Canada will be attending more than a thousand cat shows.

Currently many new breeds of cats are being accepted into the Cat Fancy. Still, however, the most popular breeds—according to a breakdown of the catteries listed in the *CATS Magazine* directory in April 1974—are Persians, Siamese, Himalayans, Burmese and Abyssinians in descending order.

Other widely accepted standard breeds are angora, Balinese and Birman longhairs; in shorthairs, British shorthairs, Havana browns, Korats, Manx, Rex, and Russian blues are the most popular. The American (or domestic) shorthair, derived from the everyday house pet, follows the Abyssinian in Cat Fancy favour.

Beyond these more or less traditional varieties, exotic new breeds are being created with increasing abandon—recklessness, some would say—in the United States and Canada and frequently receive recognition for championship showing by one or more of the various associations. Among these are the Bombays (black shorthairs resulting from crosses of black Americans and Burmese); lavenders (the lilac counterpart of the Havana brown); ocicats (off-spring of Abyssinians and other shorthair crosses); exotic shorthairs (from Persian to any shorthair crosses); Permans (Manx crossed with Persian); ragdolls (rangy Birman-patterned cats); self-longhairs (solid-colour chocolate and lilac offspring of Persian-Himalayan matings); and Somalis (from Persian with Abyssinian matings). The Sphinx—hairless cats which appeared in many shows during the late 1960s—seem to have run into some problems of heredity and are now rarely seen. Some American breeders report success in crossing the leopard cat (*Felis bengalensis*) with the American shorthair and have exhibited the offspring (called Bengals) in American cat shows.

New imported breeds which are increasingly seen are the Japanese bobtails, the Chartreaux from France and the Egyptian Mau. The angoras currently being shown are in most cases descended from recent imports from Turkey and are designated officially by most associations as Turkish angoras. Of all the traditional breeds of cats, only two can be said to be completely American: the Maine Coon, which developed from random longhair-shorthair breedings in the wild, and the Balinese, a longhaired Siamese-patterned cat with Siamese type which is said to have occurred as a mutation in the early 1950s. The Burmese got its start in the United States in the 1930s when a totally brown cat, supposedly from Burma, was mated to a Siamese and its offspring interbred until a true-breeding brown shorthaired cat was developed. Burmese have subsequently spread throughout the entire cat world. Maine Coons and Balinese, however, remain almost strictly North American breeds.

Through the accident of size, North America has become the world leader in Cat Fancy numbers and interest. Show cats here vie in quality with those from all over the world and place well in competition when shown in those countries which do not restrict their entry by quarantine regulations. Yet in many ways we still look for inspiration to the Fancies of other countries—Great Britain in particular—whose traditions are even older than ours and where the cat is even more thoroughly integrated into national life than here. The suffix 'Imp.'—imported—is borne proudly by hundreds of North American cats.

Interest in the cat is one human endeavour which successfully crosses all economic, social and national barriers and ties all cat lovers with a bond of understanding and friendship. We in North America are always aware of the great debt we owe to cat lovers of this generation and of previous ones all over the world.

From 'An Appeal to Cats in the Business of Love'

Men ride many miles,
Cats tread many tiles,
Both hazard their necks in the fray;
Only Cats, when they fall
From a house or a wall,
Keep their feet, mount their tails, and away!

THOMAS FLATMAN

Cats in Canada: Then and now

EDNA M. FIELD

The history of the cat in Canada goes back to the days of the early settlers who had a cat to guard precious grain and food supplies from rats and mice. Although there is no record of domestic cats in North America before Columbus's day, it is known that there were cats brought to North America by the Pilgrims aboard the *Mayflower*, and that descendants of these cats travelled with pioneer families to Canada. However, who can be sure that the North American Indians did not have a few pet cats of their own already here? Although the 'pioneer' cat earned his keep, he also had a warm spot in the heart of the family and was a treasured pet. Many a child cuddled a kitten in bed on a cold Canadian winter night!

Some of the longhaired Maine Coon cats from the east coast of the United States made their way into Canada with migrating families and many years and many generations later, the Maine

Coon cats were seen in some of the early cat shows. These cats were in great demand as they appealed to people who liked a long-haired cat but did not want to spend much time in grooming, for the fur is practically non-matting and so very easy to comb. These cats often grow to be very large and can weigh up to 25 pounds. They are gentle, affectionate and make ideal pets. For some un-known reason, they all but disappeared from shows in the years 1940–60, but they are gradually making a come-back and a few are seen in the shows today.

Apart from the fluffy Maine Coon, the majority of cats in the early days were shorthaired and could be found in a wide variety of colours and patterns—the lovely striped tabbies, the beautifully patched tortoiseshells and calicos, the ever-popular bi-colours and of course, the solid or self-coloured cats. Needless to say, there were a great many cats that were a mixture of any or all of these colours. Hardiness was the keynote in the early days, as it was strictly a case of survival of the fittest. The American shorthair (or domestic shorthair as it is still sometimes called) now has a championship status in cat shows and is the result of many years of selective breeding from some of the early non-pedigreed cats. The American shorthair is ever increasing in popularity in the Cat Fancy and it is not unusual to see them taking top wins in all-breed shows. They still are popular as pets, for they are strong, healthy, affectionate and intelligent—there is even a colour to suit every taste.

The many cats of unknown parentage also have a place in the cat shows, for there is a special division for unregistered cats in the household-pet class. The cats may be any colour, longhair or shorthair or 'a little bit of both', for they are judged for health, condition, beauty and temperament. They receive beautiful prizes, rosettes and trophies and this class is always one of the most popular at shows, often drawing the largest and most enthusiastic audience.

The first recorded championship cat show in Canada was held in Toronto, Ontario, in 1906, with 124 entries. Most of the pure-bred cats were Persians, but as cats did not have to be registered to enter at that time, there were also a good few entries whose proud owners considered them to be worthy of being shown, registered or not! Siamese cats did not start to appear for several more years and then were considered a great novelty. Gradually, more fanciers became interested in the newer or rarer breeds and in 1923 the largest show in North America that year was held in Vancouver, British Columbia, with 204 entries.

Although activities in the Cat Fancy were practically non-existent during the war years of 1939–45, some well-known breeders did maintain their excellent stock and continued to keep their interest until the shows resumed after the war. Within a very few years, the number of breeders had tripled and interest in cats was growing in leaps and bounds. Some fanciers imported good cats to obtain out-crosses for the blood lines and by the 1960s, Canadian breeders had established themselves firmly as some of the best in North America. By this time, serious fanciers had settled down to care-fully planned breeding programmes and soon the results were evident, for Canadian cats were holding their own in large inter-national shows. To date, Canadian breeders of Abyssinians, Burmese, Himalayans, Persians and Siamese cats are amongst the best in the world and their cats are in great demand.

Canadian shows draw large numbers of exhibitors from the USA and many international friendships have blossomed. Being part of the Cat Fancy is a great way to meet people with similar interests, to travel around making new friends and is a very rewarding hobby. Long gone is the stigma that cat-lovers were 'little old ladies in shawls' and today one finds people from all walks of life and from every type of profession finding enjoyment and relaxation in their hobby of showing, owning or just loving cats.

As in many other parts of the world, cats in Canada now come 'in all shapes, sizes and colours' and there is sure to be one to fit every choice, pocket-book and environment. Apartment dwellers (and the trend today in Canada's cities is definitely towards apart-ments) discover that in many cases they are allowed to keep a pet cat, whereas dogs are forbidden. An apartment cat therefore would, ideally, be one that would be quiet (the walls are sometimes thin), adaptable (he can use a litter-box in the bathroom just as easily as going outdoors for this chore), affectionate (he must expect to give *something* in return for his food and lodging) and as any cat-lover will agree—intelligent. He will sun himself contentedly on the window sills, amuse his people with his antics and will seek a warm, soft lap for his evening nap. More often than not, he will end up by sleeping on the foot of the bed at the end of the day. Now, what about the family who still prefers the single-home type of dwelling? This is *great* for cats! It has a front door and a back door and what cat-lover has not seen his cat peer out of one of the doors opened for him, only to find the weather not to his liking and back up into the house again in disgust? What will he do? Why, go straight to the other door and ask to be let out, quite convinced that the weather out there will be better!

Many people are discovering that there is a large selection of pure-bred cats from which to choose and there is one to suit every personality. Some of the Foreign-type shorthaired cats such as Siamese and Burmese are quite talkative and can have loud voices. For the cat-lover who likes conversation, these are just great. The Abyssinian, Manx, American shorthair and Russian blue breeds are just as lovely and playful as the Siamese and Burmese, but are less voluble. For those who prefer less action and more coat, many choose the beautiful Persian or Himalayan and take pleasure in combing the long flowing fur. Other pure-bred cats available in Canada are the shorthaired Korats, colour-point shorthairs, exotic shorthairs, Havana brown and the curly-coated Rex. In the long-haired varieties are the angora, Balinese and Birman (sacred cat of Burma). Some of the rarer breeds may be hard to find but when one considers the length of time that the cat will be a cherished family pet, the search for the right cat will be an investment. For those who do not want any of the above breeds, there is always the newly established cat that was developed in Canada—the hairless Sphinx.

Until 1960 there was no registering body in Canada and breeders had to send to the USA to register their cats in one of the American associations. However, the Canadian Cat Association was founded in that year and now has 14 affiliated clubs. After overcoming the initial growing pains, the CCA is now very active and has registered over 10,000 cats and more than 500 catteries from all parts of the United States and Canada. In addition to the CCA clubs, there are 15 active clubs affiliated with the Cat Fanciers' Association, Inc.— an international organisation and the largest cat association in the world. Most of these clubs hold championship shows annually and are spread from coast to coast across Canada, for there are clubs in Vancouver on the west coast and Halifax on the east coast—a distance of close to 3,000 miles!

Canada, as do most other countries, has to watch the problem of many unwanted cats and kittens and at present there is a programme under way to convince people to have their cats altered—neutered or spayed—so that only planned litters of kittens are born and that homes are guaranteed for the kittens. Most people now realise that it is a kindness to have their pet 'fixed' and that the cat will make a happier and more contented pet. 'Neuter and spay' clinics are appearing in many cities and financial assistance is offered to those who cannot afford the veterinarian's fee. Many of the clubs in Canada are financially supporting this project and breeders are convincing buyers of pet-type kittens that the kitten should be altered at about the age of seven months. Many veterinarians are co-operating with this effort to control the situation—many donating their service free, others charging reduced rates. This is surely a good start to the unwanted kitten situation.

In the colder parts of Canada, cats spend very little time outside in winter as their ears and feet can become frostbitten very quickly. Most pet cats are content to stay inside during the very cold weather, sunning themselves on window-sills or sitting on top of a warm radiator heater. However, some of the hardier souls will ask to be let out for a few minutes and even enjoy a short romp in the snow. Farm cats can snuggle in the warmth of the hay in barns and stables and dream of the warm spring days ahead.

There is no doubt that it is the cat or kitten's ability to adapt quickly and easily to his surroundings and conditions that has made him Canada's favourite pet. This is evident by reports from veterinarians, breeders, pet shops and manufacturers of cat food and other cat products. All report an amazing increase in cat business. It has been reported that the university courses for veterinary students have been changed to include more in-depth concentration on the cat, his habits and his welfare. No longer is it difficult to find a good 'cat man' when seeking a veterinarian, for many are now specialising in cat care. More people are attending cat shows each year—either to enter their loved pet in competition, or just to look at the beautiful exhibits. More and more people are realising that 'No home is complete without a cat'!

Australian cats

MARY BATTEN

The Australian cat differs little from its overseas counterpart—loved by some, respected by many and hated by not a few. The Australian weather is kind on the whole and for most of the year, in most parts of the continent, there is no great hardship involved in the life of the average domestic cat.

The pedigreed cat, in many instances, especially where circumstances are favourable, shares the same freedom as its domestic brother and many of our breeders, I am happy to say, keep their cats as pets, as part of a family group to be enlarged from time to time by the advent of kittens—lively, belligerent, adorable scraps which are for the most part brought up in the house and share in the happy communal life of a peacefully integrated family.

In due course these kittens make the most wonderful pets, settling into and taking over their own homes with the unfailing assurance of the kitten that has been raised in close association with man.

They take human beings very much for granted, regarding them as very large but benevolent adjuncts to their daily lives—over-sized nannies who are always there to be played with, teased, climbed on and finally cuddled up to when Mum is fed up or not available.

Of course the poor old stud cat must spend his adult life in segregation but does so quite cheerfully on the whole in well-constructed runs and houses. Whether or not our benign climate has its effect on him I could not say but he is usually a good tempered, affectionate fellow, always with a weather eye open for the approaching cat basket which will herald the arrival of female companionship of the most delightful kind.

I did on one occasion meet a Burmese gentleman who lived with his wife in his owner's home. He used to go outside when nature called him, but never as far as I could ascertain put a tail wrong in the house. Certainly there was no odour in the home which smelled a jolly sight sweeter than mine did on occasion, with calling Siamese queens on the rampage. These two Burmese raised several litters of kittens, the father never leaving his little mate and sharing all the duties of raising a family.

Most homes belonging to my 'cat' friends and acquaintances bear a striking resemblance to one another in that there is usually one chair at least, more often several, which bear the stamp of approval of the domestic cat. No matter how many scratching posts a house can boast, no matter how carefully or how assiduously these same posts have been moved from vantage point to vantage point, I think I can honestly say that no true, dyed-in-the-wool, honest-to-goodness cat-lover has not got one item of furniture which will mutely bear witness to the presence in the household of the cat.

I visited a cat-lover's home on one occasion to be shown her lounge chairs, recently covered with a plastic material but looking as though they had been gone over systematically with a nutmeg grater; each tiny pin prick in the smooth surfaces by courtesy of her precious Abyssinian!

I can well remember refurnishing my own living room with chairs and sofa covered in a patterned wool moquette. Little did I realise that each small woollen loop was obviously made to fit the needle-sharp claw of a Siamese. Within months my woollen moquette had lost its pattern in the fluff of frayed and broken loops and I took to shaving it on special occasions. The final results were

Not recognised in Britain, the Shaded Silver is very popular in many other parts of the world

A demure Chinchilla with sea-green eyes, very conscious of her beauty

not unattractive—a sort of overall woolly fuzz that one visitor at least admired as a most unusual fabric!

Have you ever noticed how inquisitive cats can be? I can never leave a cupboard door open or a ladder set up anywhere without a constant stream of 'catty' explorers picking their way daintily or bumble-footed, according to the breed, through china cups or saucepan lids or squatting gazing into space on the top steps of the ladder preparatory to taking off into the ceiling or onto the roof as the case may be.

Many years ago our garden boasted a lawn-tennis court. As we lived in a fairly busy neighbourhood I used to put the cats—four Siamese and one Burmese—on the court during the day. It was never used for tennis and creepers had been allowed to drape the wire in places, whilst underfoot the clover grew and flowered, rich and thick and fragrant. A safe and heavenly spot for cats maybe. The trouble was of course that, like the mountain, there was a fence to climb and before many moons I was alerted by the strident howls of one of my seal-point neuters who had climbed the wire and was balancing on the wooden top, picking his way like a tight-rope walker, round the rim 15 feet above the ground. He was afraid to jump and certainly had no intention of turning around and climbing down backwards with me at hand. He was telling me in no uncertain terms to get a move on and come to his rescue as he couldn't be expected to perform up here for ever, like a sooky ballet dancer.

With great difficulty I dragged our long ladder up onto the court and, climbing it, managed to coax Pete to come round, without losing his balance, to where I was standing. Plucking him off the wire I gingerly descended, accompanied by his raucous protests at being handled in such a fashion. In my relief at getting him back to ground level without injury. I completely forgot about the ladder still standing against the wire. I looked up to see a small, intent procession progressing up the ladder, like a stream of ants after sugar and onto the wire. I made a desperate leap and grasped one small, sleek body in my arms but completely missed the other two, who of course separated on reaching the top, each going in a different direction, leaving me in the middle standing stationary on what I hoped was a firmly anchored ladder. My neighbours were fairly used to my voice and the cats' answering yells by now but this was a new departure which brought most of them to their windows and

L

we played the last act to a fascinated and highly appreciative audience.

This same neuter, who was really quite a gorgeous Grand Premier, excelled in flying leaps and incredible balancing feats and one of his favourite pastimes was to spring to the top of a door, balancing on the 1½ inches of its width. He was a large, sinuous cat and of course, whilst the dark haunches and long black tail provided a somewhat unusual decoration on one side of the door, his black forepaws, sharply triangular mask, huge flaring ears and dazzlingly blue, oriental eyes draped on the other side gave more than one unwary visitor a horrible shock. It takes a very special brand of aplomb to gaze into a saturnine, slit-eyed face at such close quarters without even flinching.

Talking about aplomb, I recall Charlie, a stickler for etiquette, whose resolution to eat his meal from his enamel plate on the dining-room table never wavered. As Charlie grew older, so did his plate but a battered enamel plate, or the fact that there were guests to dinner, never in any way weakened his resolve. One could almost hear him saying, 'Don't let it worry you folks, I'm quite used to dodging the glass and silver; the candles are a bit of a nuisance but one can't win them all.' Royalty might have been present but certainly would not have deterred Charlie!

The love and tolerance most cats display towards their human owners never cease to amaze me and I have known them carry out little acts of loving kindness which argue well against the contention that animals cannot think for themselves. I have personally known one who continually braved a situation which she feared desperately, purely to ensure the safety of her particular human. We could ask no more of man than this.

Never as long as I live shall I forget my darling Siamese, Mai-ling, my first and most unforgettable introduction to the breed. She was so dainty, so captivating and so sensitive that loud noises terrified her and my vacuum cleaner sent her scampering off to hide beneath my bed. Traffic and the noises of the outside world, especially cars, horrified her. However when my husband and I returned from an outing she was always waiting at the front door and would slip through as soon as it was opened, hurrying up the pathway to the carport to meet me and to escort me back to the house; for the moment her fears laid aside in her determination to see that no harm came to me. What a loving, courageous little soul she was, ready and willing to brave unimaginable dangers for my sake.

This same Mai-ling slept in my arms each night with her exquisite small face resting against my shoulder or on my pillow. In the morning she would sit on the foot of my bed and wait for me to don my dressing gown. As soon as the belt was tied, she would leap, in one lithe and graceful movement, to my shoulder, carefully draping herself around the back of my neck, resting there like some deliciously warm and vibrant fur collar whilst I went about the business of preparing breakfast and washing up. It was only after I had made the beds that she would jump down, knowing without being told that the time had come for me to take my shower and dress. I can see her now in memory and to this day feel lapped around by her wondrous love.

I think the most intelligent cat I have ever come across was Choco, a chocolate-point Siamese. Choco undoubtedly thought for herself, living on an equal footing with her humans, sharing with them the bonds of deep affection and of mutual respect and understanding and ruling the rest of the cat family which shared the home with an iron paw encased in a dainty velvet glove.

She was an expert and meticulous mother and when on one occasion she produced one, lone kitten she decided to join forces with her daughter who was nursing a litter of six three-week-old babes in my daughter's bedroom. No matter what obstacles were placed in her way Choco continued to carry her tiny offspring into the large kitten basket and, eventually, the opposition collapsed before her persistence—as it usually did—and she was allowed to stay. The basket was full to overflowing with two mums and seven babies and care had to be taken to see that the tiny kitten didn't remain buried permanently at the bottom of the pile. It fortunately proved to be a lusty scrap and in no time at all was endeavouring to follow its older companions around. Never was there such a precocious kitten.

By the time the older ones were five weeks old, all had been transferred to a large kitten playpen in the study. Mothers and older kittens could jump or scramble out of the pen without difficulty but of course the tiny fortnight-old kitten was as yet too small even to climb out of the sleeping basket. One morning I entered the study to see the family, as usual, rushing madly helter skelter across the floor and peeped into the pen to make sure that the baby was safe. To my surprise it was not there and I couldn't see it anywhere else in the pen. With a sinking heart I knelt down on the floor, expecting to see it lying cold and perhaps injured under one of the chairs. However there was still no sign of the tiny body and, growing alarmed, I began to search the room. Choco came to help me and when she understood that I was looking for her tiny kitten she led me to a cardboard carton, a number of which stood around as play boxes and snoozing places for the cats, and jumped inside. There, nestling amongst the soft blankets with which I had thoughtfully lined this box, was the lost kitten. One or other of the mums, determined not to leave the baby behind, had lifted it out of the pen and tucked it safely out of harm's way. Every now and then one of them would hop in to feed it, closely followed by the rest of the clamouring, brawling mob. This went on until the kitten discovered that it could climb out by itself and join the rest of the family for highjinks on the floor.

Travelling throughout the Australian Cat Fancy as I do, I have met many cats, all with their own individual personalities and many of which linger in my memory. For instance there was the delightful little brown Burmese kitten which slept so close against me when last I visited Perth, West Australia, and the extremely outgoing lilac-point in Brisbane, Queensland, who insisted not only on sharing my bed herself but on bringing her two boisterous sons of four months with her. The three of them slept peacefully until 2 a.m. when they woke and decided to play.

Now in this house, as in many of our modern homes, there are no locks on the internal doors and as fast as I put her and her lively offspring out, she would leap on the door handle with all the expertise of long practice and, presto, open would swing the door and we would start all over again. Shut in another room she would raise her voice, soon to be accompanied by the kittens' plaintive squawks, to inform the by now wide-awake household of the iniquitous goings on of a certain visiting judge. For the latter part of my stay, I slept behind a door barricaded with a heavy armchair, awakened from time to time by the thump of a body landing on the door handle, followed by the sound of feet once more in contact with the floor and accompanied, I am sure, by a choice selection of Siamese swear words.

I remember on one occasion sharing my bed with a young Rex male who was attending the show from interstate. We were both visitors and we got on remarkably well. So affectionate was he that each time we drifted off to sleep he would awaken and walk all over me, rubbing his face with its crinkly whiskers into mine and purring and kneading in his joy at finding a kindred spirit so far away from home.

Smughi was a particular friend of mine. She was a seal-point lady of great elegance and distinction, who, like most of the Siamese cats I have known, adored her owner and naturally enough shared with her home, bed, chair and everything that was hers.

During the course of a long and fruitful career, Smughi gave birth to many litters which she nursed in the corner of her owner's bedroom, beside the head of the large double bed. She always paid a last visit to her owner to see that she was comfortable and preparing for sleep, slipping quietly back into her own bed and settling herself amongst her drowsy kittens. On many nights my friend would wake up to find a tiny, warm, furry body tucked in beneath her chin or resting gently against her shoulder, rising and falling contentedly with the movement of her own breathing, whilst Smughi slept peacefully with the remainder of the litter, one arm resting protectively over the little snuggling bodies. During her long lifetime she never failed to share her kittens with her beloved human whose family had grown up and left home long before.

If I have dwelt on Siamese cats it is because they have come first to my mind and perhaps because I have some slight preference here owing to a longer acquaintance with this breed. A Siamese was the first pedigreed cat I ever owned, but since then I have met and lived with many other breeds. For instance there was the blue longhair 'Woofy' who would lie on his back to be groomed, growing more grumpy as the operation proceeded until on its completion he would stalk off, tail held high and, if any other cat or kitten so much as looked at him, would deal them a brisk, but painless cuff in passing. If my daughter happened to be lying on the floor and jeered at him as went on his way, he would give her exactly the same treatment. Dear Woofy, three minutes later he was his usual sweet-tempered self. As I recall he felt the Queensland summer so badly that I used to clip his hair all over his body to one inch in length, leaving his tail and head untouched. At least he was comfortable even if he did look something like a poodle gone wrong. However it didn't take the hair long to grow and by the beginning of the autumn he invariably sported a magnificently luxuriant coat.

I can recall one very funny episode involving two exuberant

young Burmese of mine who were always filled to bursting point with the sheer joy of living and who were frequently in hot water over some riotous misdemeanour or other as a consequence.

One evening, after being kept talking on the telephone until my dinner was almost cold, I sank into my favourite arm-chair, with my plate on my knee to eat my belated meal and watch TV at the same time. Suddenly, without warning, two brown, four-legged and furry astronauts came zooming across the room, pausing in mid flight to land briefly right in the middle of my dinner, one after the other and then taking off, like twin rockets, for regions beyond! My plate did not stand up to being used as a launching pad and I suddenly found myself sitting amidst the scattered wreckage of grilled steak and salad. The lettuce and tomato found the quaintest spots on which to become attached and for one brief moment I thought I was taking part in a 'battle of the flowers' only to soon realise that 'flowers' was not the operative word and that a chunk of juicy tomato accompanied by a sly shred of well-oiled lettuce can be remarkably uncomfortable when nestling in the opening of a low V neckline! For some seconds I was speechless and could only splutter and sit like some eastern potentate garlanded by the remains of my wrecked dinner, not knowing whether to scream with mirth or rage! How my husband and daughter kept straight faces I will never understand because every time I think back and realise how absurd I must have looked I am simply rocked with mirth. It all happened so quickly! One moment I was lugubriously attacking a rapidly cooling steak, grumbling about being delayed by the phone and the next instant I was sitting speechless with an empty plate on my knee and my dinner spread all over and around me—a most artistic display of red and green.

One of my favourite stories concerns a Church of England minister and his Siamese cats. His congregation became accustomed to watching a feline procession, legs lifted high, tails elegantly aloft, picking its way daintily across the altar and soon learned to hide their surprise at the sudden appearance of several little furry shapes swinging gaily on their mentor's flowing surplice, to climb helter skelter to the top.

Weddings were particularly popular with the four-footed gang and at times they were shut out by request so that they could not steal the nuptial limelight—after all one does like to feel that one is properly married and not to a black-faced, evil-eyed Siamese cat! On these happy occasions the ceremony had the benefit of accompaniment not only of organ and congregation but also of the far-reaching and wonderfully insistent voices of several extremely indignant Siamese. They easily surmounted the tuneful clamour within and rose supreme and unchallenged in the ensuing silences.

An immediate and delightful bond exists between true cat-lovers, who of necessity become pretty shock-proof over the years. There is nothing to be compared with the average domestic cat for bringing a person down to earth. When I lived in Queensland I held many meetings and Cat Fancy parties at my home and, if you know cats, you can imagine how some of these occasions were turned into riotous affairs by the antics of mine. One afternoon tea party, which started out on quite a formal footing, was quickly reduced to a familiar free-and-easy atmosphere by the sudden appearance of the heavily laden tea trolley complete with a hefty Siamese sitting on the lower tray, busily licking the topping from a luscious cream sponge. I had wondered why it was so heavy and so difficult to push!

Siamese cats are undoubtedly more striking in appearance than the other breeds, probably because of their unique colour pattern. However, whether they be the resilient, philosophical Burmese, the gentle, soft-voiced Russian blue, the agile, independent Abyssinian, the good-natured, affectionate Rex or the glamorous, yet sweet-tempered longhair, I have come to the conclusion, through close association over the years, that cats, despite the differences of colour, breed or individual personalities are all the same—the most wonderful, wicked, beguiling and loving companions that this world has to offer.

Seen outside a factory:
REQUIRED—a cat for light mousework.

6
Miscellany

An Abyssinian over
eighty years old

A. A. DAMSTEEG

The search to establish the real origin of the Abyssinian cat has never ended. Apart from the many suggestions and myths, we know a little for certain: that the first Abyssinian appeared in Britain in 1868 and probably came from Abyssinia; that they were shown for the first time before 1874; and that they had a rather large body compared with the head and a longer and more whip-like tail as compared with the Abyssinian of today.

Nobody has ever been able up to now to find enough evidence to fix the origin of the Abyssinian cat, nor has anybody been able to prove that it has been established by mating carefully selected ticked tabbies of domestic origin. Maybe we will never be sure, but every discovery that may contribute to the knowledge of its origin is surely worth a mention.

In this respect, it will certainly be of interest to Abyssinian owners and other fanciers to learn that I have discovered an Abyssinian of more than 80 years ago. Whilst looking at some of the wild cats in the Leiden Natural History Museum, Holland, which is part of the Leiden University, I came across a small stuffed cat that carried a plate stating that this was assumed to be a *Felis domesticus* and mentioning the name of a Mr Frank.

When I saw it, I said to the man who showed me around: 'But that is an Abyssinian!' He was astonished because he had never heard of an Abyssinian cat. He told me that they had always wondered what sort of a cat it could be. The cat undoubtedly resembled very much the Abyssinian as we know it today, as to type as well as colour. Of slender build and graceful outline, it stood high on the legs and had a very long tail. The colour was extraordinarily good, of the usual black and brown, with very well ticked hairs. The dark spine line, extending to the tail, that ended in a black tip, the dark pads and the black spots above the hind pads— all were there. All the typical characteristics were present. Inside the forelegs were some dark spots and a few on the hind legs. It had a broken necklace and the underside of the chin and the places around the lips were coloured light brown.

The only faults I could detect—from the show standard point of view—were some dark spots on the legs. I am quite sure that this cat, could it have been exhibited today—would have won its CC right away and would have been an example of the ideal Abyssinian. Still there were some minor differences with the Abyssinian of today; the body was a bit larger, the tail longer and the head a bit smaller compared with the body. And we do not now see such well developed hind legs.

What could we find out about its origin? The exhibit had been sold to the museum by a Mr Frank, whose name was mentioned on the plate. Looking through the museum archives it came out that Mr Frank, a dealer in animal skulls and skeletons, had sold many between the years 1833 and 1882. The origin of this particular cat was not mentioned. It appeared also that Mr Frank travelled through different parts of the world and that he once sold to the museum antelopes from Abyssinia.

So the only thing we know for certain is that this exhibit of the Abyssinian cat came to the museum before 1882. But where did it come from?

There are two explanations. The first and most improbable is that it was one of the first Abyssinians bred in England. If so, it certainly comes up to the standard given by Harrison Weir in 1889, who mentions a large cat, and to the description of Zula, the first Abyssinian that came to England in 1868. Zula had a very long tail, while the body was large compared with the head.

The second possibility is more likely. Mr Frank was a dealer in wild animals and their skulls, and so in my opinion the museum Abyssinian was imported from another country as a wild animal. In this respect it is interesting to read Pocock's article (1907) 'On English Domestic Cats' (in the *Proc. Zool. Soc.*, London): 'Cats of the so-called Abyssinian breed may be descended, for anything I know to the contrary, from specimens of *Felis ocreata,* directly exported from Abyssinia. They are certainly not unlike some self-coloured examples of that species.'

These cats must have lived as wild animals in those days. The museum cat is therefore most likely to be a *Felis ocreata* in which the pattern is broken up and evanescent. If we look again at the picture, the outline of the cat, with its high hind legs and its long tail, it certainly looks more like a wild cat than a domestic ticked one. This Abyssinian of over 80 years old proves, in my opinion, that what we call Abyssinians today were the same more than 80 years ago and above all that the Abyssinian is not a manufactured breed as Mr Brian Vesey-Fitzgerald states in his books. And it is also most likely that the first Abyssinian cat that came from Abyssinia to England in 1868 was a wild cat, so that the Abyssinian cat could be the latest example of the domestication of *Felis ocreata* into *Felis domesticus.*

Would it not be a nice thought that what the Egyptians have done 3,000 or more years ago, the English did again not more than 100 years ago? But let us not create another myth around the origin of the Abyssinian cat.

This exhibit at Leiden is not a myth but a reality; and only realities count.

The evil spirit and the mummified cat

M. OLDFIELD MOWEY

In the year 1909 Lord Carnarvon, who was then conducting excavations in the Necropolis of the nobles of Thebes, discovered a hollow wooden figure of a large black cat, which we recognised, from other examples in the Cairo Museum, to be the shell in which a real embalmed cat was confined. The figure looked more like a small tiger as it sat in the sunlight at the edge of the pit in which it had been discovered, glaring at us with its yellow painted eyes and bristling its yellow whiskers. Its body was covered all over with a thick coating of smooth, shining pitch, and we could not at first detect the line along which the shell had been closed after it had received the mortal remains of the sacred animal within; but we knew from experience that the joint passed completely round the figure—from the nose, over the top of the head, down the back, and along the breast—so that, when opened, the two sides would fall apart in equal halves.

The sombre figure was carried down to the Nile and across the river to my house, where by a mistake on the part of my Egyptian servant, it was deposited in my *bedroom*. Returning home at dead of night, I here found it seated in the middle of the floor directly in my path from the door to the matches; and for some moments I was constrained to sit beside it, rubbing my shins and my head.

I rang the bell, but receiving no answer, I walked to the kitchen, where I found the servants grouped distractedly around the butler, who had been stung by a scorpion and was in the throes of that short but intense agony. Soon he passed into a state of delirium and believed himself to be pursued by a large grey cat, a fancy which did not surprise me since he had so lately assisted in carrying the figure to its ill-chosen resting-place in my bedroom.

At length I retired to bed, but the moonlight which now entered the room through the open french windows fell full upon the black figure of the cat; and for some time I lay awake watching the peculiarly weird creature as it stared past me at the wall. I estimated its age to be considerably more than three thousand years, and I tried to picture to myself the strange people, who, in those distant times, had fashioned this curious coffin for a cat which had been to them half pet and half household god. A branch of a tree was swaying in the night breeze outside, and its shadows danced to and fro over the face of the cat, causing the yellow eyes to open and shut, as it were, and the mouth to grin. Once, as I was dropping off to sleep, I could have sworn that it had turned its head to look at me; and I could see the sullen expression of feline anger gathering upon its black visage as it did so. In the distance I could hear the melancholy wails of the unfortunate butler imploring those around him to keep the cat away from him, and it seemed to me that there came a glitter into the eyes of the figure as the low cries echoed down the passage.

At last I fell asleep, and for about an hour all was still. Then, suddenly, a report like that of a pistol rang through the room. I started up, and as I did so a large grey cat sprang either from or on to the bed, leapt across my knees, dug its claws into my hand, and dashed through the window into the garden. At the same moment I saw by the light of the moon that the two sides of the wooden figure had fallen apart and were rocking themselves to a standstill upon the floor, like two great empty shells. Between them sat the mummified figure of a cat, the bandages which swathed it round being ripped open at the neck, as though they had been burst outward.

I sprang out of bed and rapidly examined the divided shell; and it seemed to me that the humidity in the air here on the bank of the Nile had expanded the wood which had rested in the dry desert so long, and had caused the two halves to burst apart with the loud noise which I had heard. Then, going to the window, I scanned the moonlit garden; and there in the middle of the pathway I saw, not the grey cat which had scratched me, but my own pet tabby, standing with arched back and bristling fur, glaring into the bushes as though she saw ten feline devils therein.

I will leave the reader to decide whether the grey cat was the malevolent spirit which, after causing me to bark my shins and my butler to be stung by a scorpion, had burst its way through the bandages and woodwork and had fled into the darkness; or whether the torn embalming cloths represented the natural destructive work of Time, and the grey cat was a night wanderer which had strayed into my room and had been frightened by the easily explained bursting apart of the two sides of the ancient Egyptian figure. Coincidence is a factor in life not always sufficiently considered; and the events I have related can be explained in a perfectly natural manner if one be inclined to do so.

In the eighteenth century catgut was a coarse cloth like canvas which was used for stiffening shirts and other garments. A bit later the word was applied to fiddlers and also to all stringed instruments. Now it may be that long, slender cord made from the dried intestines of sheep and other animals which is known to violinists, tennis players and surgeons or perhaps a perennial herb found in the eastern United States.

GILEAN DOUGLAS, *Cats in our language*

Egyptian statuette (Original in Belgium museum)

An Abyssinian cat over 80 years old, seen in a museum in Holland

Engraving after Gottfried
Mind

Charcoal drawing by
Steinlen

The cat in art

MICHAEL WILSON

From an aesthetic point of view the cat is a work of art in itself. No other animal has those well-known qualities of superb physical grace, vitality and agility in quite such abundant measure, while the aura of mystery that surrounds the cat belongs to it alone.

Small wonder, therefore, that over many centuries it has attracted artists as an intriguing subject for their work, quite apart from the affinity that has always existed between cats and creative artists in general. This affinity may be traced back to the earliest representations of cats that have come down to us—those from ancient Egypt.

Somewhere about the year 8,000 BC, the cat—if we are to believe Rudyard Kipling—'Walked By Itself' voluntarily out of the mists of prehistory to the fireside of man, and became his companion and guest. It repaid his hospitality by keeping down the vermin that consumed the all-important, life-sustaining grain and this was duly appreciated. It was especially appreciated in Egypt, at that time the granary of the civilised world, where in time man's original respect for the cat became religious worship and the cat itself was identified with the goddess of love and the moon, Bast, Bastet or Pasht. Hence all the many wonderful cat idols and figurines that bear witness to this devotion. But these are nevertheless official religious art, in a sense the equivalent of medieval statuettes of saints. Far more interesting are the tomb wall-paintings in which cats are shown joining in the daily life and activities of humans—feeding, playing and in more than one case apparently accompanying men on hunting expeditions in a role similar to that of the modern retriever dog. Such paintings prove that the cat's place in Egyptian life was a dual one; not only was it sacred, it was also to the Egyptians a delightful domestic companion, beloved and cosseted, and at death bewailed, mummified and entombed with miniature splendour. Numerous cat mummies have survived, but it is in the tomb paintings (most of them Theban and dating from *c.* 1630 BC onwards) that the Egyptian cat truly lives on.

The feline Golden Age may be said to have ended when the Romans totally subjugated Egypt and in the process stamped out the ancient cult of Bast, which they regarded as subversive. To the Romans themselves, as also to the Greeks, cats might seem to have been of little account, if we are to judge by the comparatively few classical representations that have come down to us. Of these, the best-known example is probably a mosaic from Pompeii showing a tabby cat in the act of catching a large bird, but even this seems to be Alexandrian in origin and it is worth noting that not a single cat bone has ever been unearthed at either Pompeii or Herculaneum. This mosiac apparently served as a model for several other similar ones elsewhere within the Roman Empire; most of them are of very inferior artistic quality, which again may indicate that no live models were readily available. The original mosaic is well executed, the cat being lively and realistic, though the subject matter might be thought disagreeable. However, although the artist may not himself have been a Roman, it is entirely typical of the Roman character that the mosaic should show the more savage side of a cat's nature. Nothing is gained by shutting one's eyes to this fact of cat life and the artist of integrity has never done so.

It is nevertheless dangerous to make sweeping pronouncements on the status of cats under the Romans or indeed at any other period in early history. A completely different impression of the Roman attitude is conveyed by a number of sculptured tomb portraits of the first and second centuries AD to be found in Northern Europe, especially France, in which pet cats are shown with their deceased owners. The Roman provinces were far-flung and in principle it is true to say that the cat still enjoys more popularity in Northern Europe than it does in the countries of the Mediterranean.

Similarly, representations of cats in Greek art are confined to a mere handful of vase paintings and sculptured reliefs that do little to shed significant light on the classical Greek attitude to the cat, except that on the whole it too does not seem to have been particularly sympathetic. What is probably the best-known example is an Athenian relief of *c.* 450 BC featuring young men apparently urging a cat and a dog to fight.

In medieval Europe the cat's normal role had reverted to that of humble vermin exterminator, in which it remained popular with the peasantry. This is attested to by the large number of carved stone capitals, wooden misericords and bench ends showing it as a rat and mouse catcher, often with considerable humour. Yet its ancient past could not be forgotten and now indeed became a dangerous burden. For organised religion, unable to absorb or destroy completely all the deep-rooted pagan beliefs centering on sun and moon worship, denounced them collectively as Satanism and witchcraft, with which the unfortunate cat—because of its Egyptian background, its ancient connection with the moon goddess and its natural mystery—was inevitably associated. Thus in certain religious paintings, mostly Italian, the cat does actually represent evil personified, the devil himself, as in a well-known late fifteenth-century 'Last Supper' by Ghirlandaio, in which it sits immediately behind Judas. In at least two paintings of the Virgin and Child in which the latter holds a goldfinch, symbol of the Christian spiritual life, a cat is also introduced probably as a representative of the darker side of man's nature.

On occasion the cat plays a symbolic part in paintings dealing with the life of the Virgin Mary. These allusions, often obscure, are seldom so marked as in a celebrated sixteenth-century 'Annunciation' by Lorenzo Lotto at Recanati, in which a large tabby darts away in fear both of the descending Archangel and of the gesturing hand of a cloud-borne God the Father. This cat perhaps personifies the old evil giving way to the promise of the new dispensation, nor can we overlook the connection between the Virgin Mary herself and the pagan version of the virgin goddess, with which—under her various names of Pasht, Artemis, Diana and others—the cat had always been associated.

Despite the hostility of the religious authorities, which sometimes became active persecution, the gradual rehabilitation of the cat is marked above all by its inclusion in religious art not as a symbol of evil or paganism but often apparently simply for its own sake. One of the first instances of this new attitude is an early fourteenth-century fresco in the lower church of St Francis at Assisi; in a scene of the Last Supper a disgruntled cat flattens its ears in disgust at a dog which is licking with relish a plate put down on the floor by servants. Though Judas sits nearby there is apparently no symbolic link with the cat. It appears also entirely as a domestic animal in certain illuminated manuscripts of the fifteenth-century Flemish and French schools.

Opposition to cats on religious grounds was doubtless effectively eroded by the basic humanity of Renaissance ideas. The new thinking is summed up in the various engaging studies by Leonardo da Vinci for a painting (apparently never completed) of the Virgin and Child with a cat, in which the well-known reluctance of cats to participate in any activity that they consider foolish and undignified is shown with accuracy and humour, and without any obvious symbolism. In fact the various original symbolic attributes of the cat gradually faded from the minds of artists, and we find that by the sixteenth century the animal is regularly introduced, unhampered by obscure symbolic references, into all types of religious painting, culminating in the great Biblical feast scenes of Tintoretto and Veronese in which it makes several appearances.

One other symbolic cat should be especially noticed here, because the picture in which it appears is so familiar, though probably the symbolism is less so. The picture is Dürer's famous engraving of Adam and Eve, in which the cat sitting at their feet in the immediate foreground seems contented enough. Yet the inference is that as soon as the fatal apple of discord has been tasted the pent-up forces of evil will be loosed upon the world, an event to be symbolised by the cat's leaping onto the mouse which for the moment is playing happily nearby. Another interpretation is that the cat, both in this picture and in others, represents a kind of primitive but all-seeing wisdom with foreknowledge of both good and evil and certainly this particular cat, though apparently so somnolent, has a characteristic air of withdrawn but total awareness.

It is interesting to note that in taking Dürer's engraving as their model for different versions of the Fall, other artists took over the cat as well, and it becomes a fairly constant feature of this scene until the end of the seventeenth century. But by that time it had entirely lost its symbolic significance and was just another creature in a well-stocked Paradise. Particularly engaging examples of cats in the Garden of Eden are those engraved by Theodore Gallé, Bloemart and Jan Brueghel (who produced several painted versions with different cats in each). Enchanting visions of the same, from which Adam and Eve are entirely excluded, have been painted by the nineteenth-century German artist Adolf Oberländer (in which the cat shares its saucer of milk with two mice) and, in our own day, by Eden Box whose 'Co-existence Tree' is a haven for both cats and birds.

In secular art, the principal origins of all those cosy domestic fireside scenes and genre pictures featuring cats, which are still being produced today, are to be found in the work of the seventeenth-century Dutch school. The comfortable domesticity of those well-loved interiors, riotous gatherings and scenes of daily life is many times emphasised by the presence of a cat, often portrayed with an insight that is lacking in the work of the greatest masters. For such cats one turns not to Rembrandt, whose extremely poor attempts at showing them perhaps reflects a personal dislike of the species, but to artists such as Jacob Jordaens, Jan Steen or Nicolas Maes.

Portraits of human sitters shown in the company of cats probably begin (if one ignores the Egyptian tomb paintings) with the 1560 painting of the Genoese Admiral Giovanni Andrea Doria, formerly attributed to Titian. The cat, an enormous tabby, is said to have been a great favourite with the Admiral and to have accompanied him on all his voyages. Better known in England is the portrait of about 1600 by De Critz showing the third Earl of Southampton with his black and white cat, which supposedly visited him in the Tower of London where he was imprisoned for his part in the Essex rebellion. Another famous, though later, English portrait is Hogarth's wonderful 'Four Graham Children' (1742) with their cat, which peers hopefully over a chair-back at a caged bullfinch. (This attitude is curiously paralleled by Goya, whose young 'Don Manuel Osoria de Zuñiga' leads a pet magpie that is closely eyed by no less than three large cats.)

A long tradition of French portraits with cats also begins in the eighteenth century. In those by Greuze, Perroneau and Mercier the animals for the first time seem to reflect the personalities of the humans. Also for the first time, these artists deliberately use cats to introduce a note of the voluptuous into portraiture, a technique later developed to its highest pitch by certain members of the Impressionist school, notably Renoir, whose ability to capture on canvas the sensual aspect of cat-human relationships has never been surpassed; one can almost hear his cats purring.

Complete equality between cats and humans in portraiture was probably first attained by that great nineteenth-century cat artist Theodore Steinlen, whose affections seem to have been about equally divided between his little daughter Colette and the Montmartre cats with which he was habitually surrounded; both Colette and the cats have become famous through Steinlen's various posters and graphic works. But a similar equality was also achieved on the other side of the world by the Japanese artist Kuniyoshi (1798–1861) in his printed portraits of celebrated actors and courtesans with their cats. In Japan the cat has always held a special place in the general affections of the people and has been championed by numerous artists, of whom Kuniyoshi was undoubtedly the most sympathetic. It is said that cats outnumbered students in his studio and his quick sketches of cats alone, though drawn with the utmost economy of line and detail, are none the less invested with inimitable humour and affection.

It is a reasonable assumption that the likenesses of cats which appear in portraits with humans are mostly if not all authentic. Nor is this fact confined only to portraiture. For instance, what is un-doubtedly the same cat appears in a number of the paintings, mostly religious in theme, by the sixteenth-century Da Ponte family of Bassano. Here was evidently an honoured family pet that did duty as a model when required. And in Tintoretto's version of the Last Supper at Venice we are confronted in the foreground by a gigantic bob-tailed ginger tabby, standing on its hindlegs with head and forepaws thrust inquisitively into a basket. This is such a very dis-tinctive animal that Tintoretto must surely have known it personally. Beautiful studies of cats, obviously taken from life, occur in a number of still-life paintings by eighteenth-century French artists, notably Chardin and Desportes.

But the true cat portrait, in which the cat appears entirely alone and in its own right, is of two kinds, the first being that of named or otherwise identified cats Examples of this type are rare before the nineteenth century. No doubt the most generally familiar—and also one of the earliest—is the 1661 engraving by Wenceslaus Hollar of the Grand Duke of Muscovy's cat, which shows the mask only. The animal has a most penetrating gaze, with a curious discrepancy in the eyes that suggests possible blindness in one of them. At all events it seems the face of this cat, evidently celebrated in its day, was sufficiently unusual as to cause Hollar (always meticulous about detail) to emphasise in his French caption to the engraving that, despite appearances to the contrary, he has given us *le vray portrait* of the animal. (It is, however, remarkably similar to an even earlier Hollar engraving of 1646, showing the face of another cat said to be his own; this animal is captioned, in both Czech and German, 'A good cat which never steals'.)

The second category of portrait, that of cats unnamed and unidentified though taken from life, is of course far larger and ranges from complete and finished likenesses down to sketches and studies. In fact some of the best attempts at cat portraiture have been made in the form of swift sketches rather than of completed works, for, owing to the refusal of most cats to hold a suitable pose except one of their own choosing (usually one of simulated sleep), the artist must take the cat as he finds it. This explains why artists who are without innate sympathy for cats almost invariably fail to paint, draw or sculpt them convincingly, for without that sympathy there cannot be the requisite amount of patience needed to create a successful portrait.

This tradition of the quick study, the snapshot of the cat in all its various elusive and delightfully contorted positions, goes back in Western European art at least as far as Villard de Honnecourt (working *c.* 1235), who has left a sketch of a thin-faced, rat-tailed creature that seems to typify the cat of medieval times. The cat sketches of Leonardo, which exist quite apart from his preliminary studies for the Virgin and Child painting, have often been reproduced. However, a significant corpus of such sketches does not seem to exist before the eighteenth century, when the trickle at last becomes a noticeable stream that flows on to our own day. Especially notable are the studies by the French artists Watteau, Oudry, Greuze, Géricault, Delacroix and Steinlen and also those by the Japanese Hiroshige and Hokusai, in addition of course to Kuniyoshi.

More finished portraits of unidentified cats are exceptional before the nineteenth century, when they often became part of the output of those artists who now began to specialise in animal painting,

such as William Huggins of Liverpool (1820–84). More import-
antly, certain artists became specialists in cat portraiture; of these
the best-known is the Dutch-born Henriette Ronner (1821–1909),
whose work reveals considerable affection for, and understanding of
cats. Nevertheless, some of her paintings show traces of a sentimentality which brings them perilously close to the borderline of
commercial cat art, by which is meant all those tedious genre
scenes, involving kittens rather than full-grown cats, that ever since
the mid-nineteenth century have been one of the staple products of
the greetings-card and chocolate-box industries. For this reason
one may well prefer the work of an earlier cat specialist, Gottfried
Mind of Basle (1768–1874), known as the 'Raphael of the cats' (a
title apparently bestowed on him by Madame Vigée Lebrun), in
whose work no trace of sentimentality exists. Accounted by the
world as simple-minded, and shamelessly exploited, Mind cared
for nothing but the cats with which he was surrounded and which he
drew and painted constantly with insight, sympathy and skill.

In modern times the cat has not lacked appreciative interpreters.
Again it is the French school that seems to lead the field, with such
notable twentieth-century cat artists as the painters Jacques Nam and
Erté, and the sculptor Sandoz. Tsuguharu Fujita is a particularly
interesting example of a Japanese-born, French-domiciled artist com-
bining in himself a fascinating Franco-Japanese approach to cat
portraiture. And in Britain the cat-filled landscapes and interiors
of Eden Box have a mysterious and hypnotic quality that is not only
unforgettable but is also peculiarly in tune with cat character.

Any discussion of the cat's place in illustration must sooner or
later lead us to confront the problem of cats shown dressed and
behaving as human beings. This is a convention that goes as far
back as Egyptian times, for at least one tomb painting shows a cat
as a goose-herd, standing upright and brandishing a stick. But,
as is well known, the cat of all animals is probably the least amen-
able to circus-type training and hence the really successful and
memorable cats of literature are undoubtedly those which the artist
concerned has interpreted for us with true insight into cat character,
imposing upon them the minimum of human attributes. For example, the cats of the nineteenth-century French illustrator Jean
Isadore Gérard (known as Grandville) retain their essential catness,
even though fully clothed in the height of Second Empire fashion,
and the same is true of the kimono-clad cats occasionally drawn by
Kuniyoshi and his contemporaries. On the other hand it is certainly

not true of the cats of Louis Wain, who many people would regard as the cat artist *par excellence.* In the first place, Wain's single-minded devotion to cats soon became an obsession linked with genuine mental disturbance; in the second, despite an apparently genuine love for cats, he continuously portrayed them with human expressions on their faces and in costumes and situations which are entirely and (to a cat) degradingly human. It is true, however, that his straightforward sketches of prize-winning cats are exquisite, while many of his semi-serious drawings are both colourful and appealing.

It is perhaps worth noting here that Beatrix Potter seems to have been a rare example of an artist who has habitually included cats in her general output, while not feeling personally attached to them, and in so doing has succeeded in depicting them reasonably well. Her pictures of cats are, however, by no means invariably successful, and it is therefore significant that, as her diaries reveal, she was less sympathetic towards them than towards almost any other animal.

The supreme cat of modern illustrative art is surely that delightful marmalade creature Orlando, who undoubtedly owes his well-deserved popularity to the twin facts that, firstly, he has a real-life prototype also called Orlando and, secondly, that his adventures are both written and illustrated by the same gifted creator—who understands cats.

The story of the cat's representation in art is as long as the animal's own history, and has here been only very lightly sketched. But cat-lovers who choose to follow up the story and to fill in some of the details for themselves will find it a fascinating and indeed inexhaustible one.

Photographing cats

ANNE CUMBERS

If you possess a little more than average patience with animals and are fond of cats in particular, then to photograph them can be a delightful pastime. A certain tenacity of purpose is also a help as results do not always come quickly. In fact it is wise not to set yourself a time limit. It could be one, two, or even three hours before you are satisfied and often the best shot comes just as you are about to give up. My family is now used to my late home-comings. In the beginning, if I was expected home by tea time and arrived three hours later, there was consternation. Now if I say a time they double it and don't worry. I might also add that it can be quite tiring both for the photographer and for the owner of the cat. My back muscles have strengthened I am sure, as now I rarely suffer with backache, but I am always aware that my helper must be feeling the strain.

A cat is pretty mobile. Either he is inquisitive and wants to explore, or nervous and needs to hide, affectionate and insists on rubbing around any handy object, or playful and flies after his toy. He has to be cajoled and enticed back into a suitable position.

No one is ever cross with a cat for he is a law unto himself. A dog can be commanded to sit or lie down. A child can be told what is required, but there is no explaining to a cat. It is just a case of awaiting his lordship's pleasure!

All this takes a good deal of energy on the part of your helper and unless her enthusiasm is as great as your own she may not take kindly to being reduced to a physical wreck just for a few photographs. I must say most hide any discomfort they feel and share my sense of achievement at a good result. One can manage alone and for some types of picture this is best, but usually an extra pair of hands is much appreciated.

Before I go any further a few words on equipment might be useful. It need not be elaborate. Each has his preference in cameras. But I prefer to use a twin-lens reflex and compose my picture looking down in the view finder. Also I find it easier for focusing more exactly. A fairly powerful flashgun, some simple backgrounds, a few toys and plenty of fast films should be all that is necessary. Floodlighting is not suitable to my mind for this sort of photography being too static and hot and alarming for the cats. One must be prepared to move around and shoot wherever the cat decides to pose.

Use a fast shutter speed, 1/500 second, together with a fast film so that you can stop down to f16 or f22. This is to get as much depth of field as possible. A cat is a very small subject and you need to get up very close for it to fill the view finder. This means your depth of field is limited unless you stop down well. I automatically focus on the eyes, and hope that the nose and body will also be sharp but if the light is poor and I have to open up a little the body might be fuzzy. That is why, for the sharpest results I find my next piece of equipment so useful—the flash gun, strong enough to use as a bounce flash. This gives a soft overall lighting without hard shadows and a very fast exposure—perhaps 1/1000 second— to freeze the antics of a playful kitten or a promenading cat. Working in an average modern room with a light ceiling and good reflecting surfaces f16 or even f22 and a fast film give good results. Thus you can be sure of getting the whole cat in focus and many sharp action shots.

Photographing out of doors gives greater scope for more beautiful backgrounds and natural pictures. On a good bright day—not necessarily very sunny because the shadows are a menace—and with plenty of time to wander around quietly with your subject in a lovely garden there should be many opportunities for super pictures. It does not always turn out like that of course. Even in the most beautifully kept garden there are glory holes and cat-owners are not always fond of gardening, or have time for it. You may be sure that his lordship's favourite spot is not the most picturesque! It may be on a ledge near the dustbin or in the cool under a shed, or round by the compost heap where he watches for mice. Even so, given time and patience, you will no doubt get something interesting.

However, if it is portraiture you are after and want to show the cat off at its best, indoor photography is more likely to achieve this —and there is no risk of puss disappearing over the garden fence and not coming home till supper time! I remember I once had to photograph a special pet cat for a special purpose and when I arrived at 10.30 a.m. the owner was in distress because junior had let the said pet out for a walk before breakfast. We spent many hours calling and waiting, drinking cups of coffee, calling again but, no luck, no photographs! I guess he was having a good giggle under a bush in the next-door garden.

Indoors the background is more easily controlled. When I go into other people's homes, however, I never know what the conditions are going to be like. I take a quick look around the available rooms and decide on one with plain emulsioned walls or a quiet attractive wallpaper. Perhaps a kitchen with a suitable expanse of wood panelling or tiling, or a lounge with a plain covered settee, may suggest a good background. But if nothing is suitable I am always prepared because I take a simple portable background around with me in the car.

I purchase two stiff art cards, about 40 inches by 30 inches and some wide adhesive tape to join them together and act as a hinge. Thus they can be folded flat for travelling and opened up to 90° or so and propped against a wall or chair legs to form a platform and background. These cards can be obtained in various colours and are cheap to replace if they become soiled with muddy paw marks. A warm blanket and other material can also be arranged over them for a different effect. Some cats settle better on a cosy surface. In fact I have used an electric blanket, switched on low, to encourage a group of active kittens to settle down a bit, especially if they are babies. I might add here that it is not advisable to have this arrangement too high off the ground, in case the kittens take a flying leap off to the floor below. Two helpers here are better than one—and do arrange a few cushions around to soften the fall of a gay adventurer.

When this has all been set up it does not necessarily mean it will be used. I often finish on the other side of the room where the model has decided he likes it better. This can be in the most unsuitable place but even then thought must be given to the background. It must be kept uncluttered and often perhaps a move to the left or right or a higher perch may make quite a difference to the finished picture.

On arrival for a photographic session I am perhaps told that Tiggy is asleep upstairs on the bed or sunning himself somewhere, blissfully unaware of the fun and games ahead. I ask if I may go where he is and quietly get a shot or two before he is conscious of my presence.

Cats are very much individuals and vary greatly in how they react to a stranger. Some are self-assured and greet you quite happily, while others are very nervous and shy. Always approach a new model with a gentle and friendly voice and most will be won over pretty soon. Certainly to thrust a camera at him too suddenly is asking for trouble. A really frightened cat does not forget quickly. I once spent a whole day trying to photograph a notoriously nervous cat and did *not* succeed. We tried everything to soothe him and give him confidence but he spent the whole day in various dark hide-outs and refused even his owner's overtures.

Others, of course, are friendly and inquisitive from the beginning; some extremely so, wanting to spend their time rubbing round your legs and singing, which makes photographing from a good angle somewhat tricky.

Some like to roll, some want to play and many, if they feel embarrassed as I am sure they do, prefer to appear nonchalant and insist upon vigorously attending to their ablutions!

This is not altogether a bad thing as at least they are 'done roaming' for a bit and a few interesting shots may be obtained of the process. I find that, perhaps when the ears have been thoroughly washed, they may pause and take a good long thoughtful look at you whilst they are deciding which part next needs attention. I have on occasion, when my model has been excessively active, put a tiny spot of butter on his paw to encourage this industry. It does not always work but it is worth trying. Whatever their temperament they get used to you and the idea in time. Then, of course, boredom may set in and with it comes the dreaded hunched position.

The type of pose you are aiming for depends entirely on the breed of cat you are photographing. The longhaired variety needs to show his gorgeous coat and ruff, his short body, chubby legs and paws and his flattish profile. Get his owner to attract him over your shoulder so that you really see his large, round wide-open eyes. Similarly, with the British shorthaired cat, his cobby body, round face and short tail must be shown to advantage.

With the Siamese and foreign types encourage a long elegant outline emphasising the long whip tail and the long straight profile. This breed is seldom still and so it is a case of watching in your viewfinder to catch the most graceful attitude as it appears: tall and slim for Siamese and foreign, short and cobby for longhaired and British shorthairs.

The condition of the eyes and of the coat shows up very clearly in a photograph and so it is wise to watch these things. Keep a piece of silk or velvet handy when photographing shorthaired cats and a brush and comb for longhaired, so that attention may be given in mid-session, if necessary because there has been a lot of handling. I need hardly say that the winter is the best time to get the good coats. The longhaired cats seem twice their size when in prime condition, which, especially in a mild winter, may only be for about six weeks in the year.

A cat show is a possible place to get close-up shots of beautiful pedigree cats, which have had a lot of extra-special care lavished upon them. Probably a week before, they have been carefully shampooed and on each day after they have been lovingly groomed so that on the day they look absolutely perfect.

There they are in their pens. They cannot escape and they look at their best for all to admire. However, there are a few snags to show photography. Firstly, of course, it is not allowed whilst judging is in progress and when that is over, the public flock around to admire and exclaim. This makes for congestion around the pens. Then, of course, they are behind bars and the owners have to be found and approached to open the door of the pen. This often unsettles the cat as they expect a little fussing and want to greet their owner. So one must be patient while they settle down again.

If it is a small cat being photographed it may well be possible to get a shot through the door without bars spoiling the picture. But with a large Persian the most one can hope for is a head study. On the other hand it is quite likely that by this time he is tired and sleepy and will pose for you without moving, but guard against the bored, sleepy look. A gentle squeak, or a toy quickly introduced, may give you an alert expression for a moment.

It is not often there is sufficient available light in the hall and so a flash has to be used—and cats can be very nervous on the day of a show. Flashlight also often has an effect on the appearance of the eyes in the resulting photograph.

All in all, I would say it is quite a chancy business to get a good photograph at a cat show. It is possible to get a few real beauties but disappointments are also very likely. I much prefer to work at leisure in quieter surroundings.

It should be very much easier to get some lovely pictures of your own cat as you can choose the moment. He is quite relaxed and will not get fussed with you as everything and everyone is familiar. You know his favourite spots and his funny ways. You suddenly see him looking absolutely gorgeous against a perfect background. You are probably in the middle of cooking lunch but you hastily reach for your camera and quickly approach a vantage point from which he shows up really well and, just as you are about to release the trigger, your youngest comes bounding up and greetings are exchanged. Or if not that, then puss will choose that very moment to decide it is time for a short nap and will curl up with his back towards you. By then there is a suspicious smell of burning and the lunch is ruined!

Your husband may be a keen photographer and you beg him to have a go. Eventually he will, but if the cat does not oblige and pose in five minutes he is back in the garage or wherever. I would not like to be too emphatic on this point—there are always exceptions—but it is pretty safe to say that women have more patience in this kind of situation than do men.

Many enjoyable hours can be spent photographing the antics of kittens and young cats. With a few playthings, pieces of string, balls on elastic, cotton reels, they are making pictures for you all the time. Keep the background clear and watch. Too many kittens skipping around are inclined to confuse the scene, so isolate one or two and get some shots with real movement in them. To take a group of kittens some effort has to be made to organise them, otherwise there may be more backs than fronts. Perhaps it is better to wait until they have tired a little and are more willing to be put in their places.

Queens with their litters are much easier as they naturally want to keep together. The mothering instinct of a cat gives so many opportunities for appealing photographs and kittens aged three or four weeks are not very mobile. It is fascinating to catch their first attempts at play. When they are older, this is the time for action photographs and it is fun to get someone to play with a young Burmese with a ball on elastic. It is amazing how high he will jump and what graceful poses he will strike. Get ready with your flash and shoot as fast as you can. Some of the results will be headless but with luck you will capture some fantastic attitudes.

There are many ways of attracting a cat's attention to get an alert expression. His hearing is very acute—when he wants to hear —and it is good to have a repertoire of small noises to arouse his curiosity. Tiny squeaks and barks or meows, a squeaky toy, a nail scratching or a tap on a window. All must be gentle. Loud noises at the worst frighten him, at the least make him flatten his ears. None will work if repeated! A long piece of dried grass will attract the eyes and often guide them in the desired direction and a catnip toy will induce some sentimental expressions.

Children with their pets are another source of picture-making. This has to be approached carefully. I find if a little child is about he often wants to be in on it and have his picture taken with his cat. He will grab his pet and hold him in a tight and awkward way and poor puss gets very cross and shoots off in a huff leaving a tearful child behind. A little tact in the beginning could avoid this happening. Here the child has to be managed as well as the cat and later on a play session might be engineered when both child and cat are behaving naturally. Opportunities will then arise for delightful studies. It is different, of course, with older children. Once you get past their first stage of self-consciousness they will play gently with their cats and kittens and be quite a help in getting a required result.

Dogs and cats, if they have been brought up together, often become tremendous pals and are happiest when sleeping or playing together and give one more time-consuming way of making appealing pictures.

In fact there are so many ways of photographing cats that I find it a never-ending source of enjoyment, worth all the time and patience expended.

A picture of feline grace

A fairy-like Chinchilla kitten surveying the world through black-rimmed sea-green eyes

A Colourpoint with pale coat and seal points; an excellent example of a man-made breed

Feline flood rescues

WALDO CARLTON WRIGHT

When tropical storm Agnes did a backlash over Eastern Pennsylvania, angry muddy water swept down the Susquehanna River. Cows
and sheep were swept from pastures. Barns floated away. Entire
towns were inundated, houses forced off their foundations, walls
collapsed. But what happened to 20,000 cats in Wyoming Valley?

In and around Wilkes Barre, Civil Defence headquarters began
warning families to leave their homes Thursday 22 June. Many
moved in with friends on higher ground or were taken to rescue
centres. With them they took their pets, dogs, cats, canaries.

But many others who had sat tight through other flood warnings,
refused to move out. They had survived other high water in the
valley. Some noticed that their pets acted strangely—would keep
running upstairs, crawling on beds, on dresser tops. Even making
their way to the attic.

Friday morning, 23 June, volunteers piling sandbags on the dikes along River Street in Wilkes Barre, were told to abandon the effort. A second wave of high water was surging down the already overflowing stream. Before most families could drive from their homes, this wave rushed over the dikes. Cats caught out of doors scrambled up trees.

Rescue boats, hastily brought in, carried families from their already flooded homes, often from upstairs windows. In these hurried departures there wasn't time to find the family cat.

Those who took their pets along in the boats discovered on reaching high ground in the lobby of the airport, under the grandstand of the race track, or in schools and churches, there was no place for animals, sometimes only standing room for people.

One radio station managed to continue on the air, broadcasting directions to the displaced, where they could find shelter, food, dry clothing. This station also reported that animals were being taken care of at the SPCA shelter on Fox Hill.

All day people carried in their frightened pets. By that evening over 600 cats and dogs were crowded into all the available cages. A communal room, set aside for cats, was filled with mewing, bewildered pets.

All day the phone in the SPCA shelter jangled, bringing word of pets, abandoned in the rush from the raging waters. Would the shelter send someone to rescue them?

That night when all available spaces were filled, the lights blacked out, the phones went dead. Candles were lit and the work of housing, feeding and comforting the frightened animals went on.

By Saturday morning the walls of the shelter were bulging with hungry, frightened pets. A nearby garage was commandeered, rows of cages were stacked three high. Part-time girl volunteers were enlisted to work full time around the clock, with the cleaning and feeding.

Through Civil Defence word of the plight of the shelter reached the Women's SPCA of Philadelphia. Appeals went out to the American Humane Society, the Society for Animal Rights in New York and many branches of the Pennsylvania SPCA.

A ton of pet food arrived Sunday afternoon from the Humane shelter in Scranton. Wire cages were sent from Philadelphia. The Cleveland Armory Fund for Animals sent needed humane cat traps.

Even while the entire length of historic Wyoming Valley was a brown boiling lake, many animals were rescued by the boats patrolling the flooded streets. One cat jumped from a garage roof, swam to a boat, clawed her way aboard.

Others were less sure of safety in a boat. A woman resident of the Sterling Hotel in downtown Wilkes Barre carried her Persian champion with her when she crawled into the launch that was taking off those stranded in the hotel. When the motor started the cat became frightened, tried to jump out. The woman was badly scratched but managed to quiet her pet, bring it to the shelter.

Before the water had drained from South Wilkes Barre, a student from Wilkes College came to the shelter for help. He had left his two cats in styrofoam picnic chests in his apartment. Would someone help him bring out his hungry pets. The cats were found still floating around the flooded room. They were brought to the shelter and held until the student reclaimed them.

In a ten-day period 606 homeless animals had found refuge in the shelter. About half of them were cats, all colours, all breeds: Siamese, Persians, Manx, Angoras, Maine Coons, and just plain cats.

As soon as they were permitted access to the flooded areas, the SPCA rescue trucks started on their missions of mercy to find stranded animals. They had long lists of houses where the owners had reported pets left behind.

Two girls manned each truck. It was rough going through the debris-littered streets. Destruction everywhere. Everywhere the stench of sewage, all overcast with slippery mud that made walking almost impossible. In some streets houses were piled up like children's blocks against trees. Garages had toppled over. Walls had collapsed, strewing broken furniture. Among all this, dead cows, bloated sheep washed down from farms upstream.

Cats were spotted still clinging to roofs or lodged in the branches of trees. These were lowered by rescue poles, placed in cages in the truck. Entering abandoned homes was more hazardous. Often rescuers got inside through a broken window. Sometimes it was impossible to reach a stranded cat or dog. Then a week's supply of food and uncontaminated water was left.

One of the first animals rescued was a cat in an upstairs bedroom. She had floated on a mattress while giving birth to four kittens. They had tumbled off and drowned.

In their hurried departure a family from Forty Fort could not find Ginger and her four kittens. Four days later the crew from the SPCA shelter saw something moving in the top of a rose trellis of this same house. There they found Ginger and three of her kittens. One had fallen off and drowned.

Many of the rescued animals were in pathetic condition. One cat was coated with black oil. The SPCA attendants did what they could to clean it. But it continued to lick its fur which apparently poisoned it.

For days the Gateway apartments was completely under water. Sixteen days after the flood a cat from there was found clinging to the roof of a nearby building. When she was taken down, her claws were completely worn down, and the insides of her legs were raw. Having been without food or water for all that time, she was almost dead. At the shelter she was treated and fed, but her claws have not yet grown back.

During the emergency, 1,068 cats were saved from drowning and starvation by the efforts of the rescue team of ten girls and two young men of the SPCA shelter, plus all the help that came in from so many humane-minded agencies.

Starved for days, many of the cats had forgotten how to swallow, or had acquired extremely sore throats. They had to be retrained by touching a finger wet in milk on their parched tongues. Gradually they would get the idea and would eat small amounts of their favourite food.

Many suffered from exposure and poisoning from the filth that clung to their fur. As was to be expected, the pedigree cats showed more signs of hysteria than did the alley and free-roaming cats.

Sometimes rescue came too late. There were 14 Siamese in an attic, four adults and ten kittens, two of them mother cats. They had been there for three weeks when found by the SPCA. All died.

At no time during the rescue operation was there a shortage of food, water or medicine.

According to Miss Ruth M. Jones, executive director of the Fox Hill shelter, cats are better equipped to take care of themselves than dogs because they can often climb to safety and because they adjust better to temporary quarters. There were no instances of a cat going berserk, as did a few dogs.

Within a few weeks, as the displaced families were moved into temporary homes or returned to their former homes, many came to the shelter to claim their pets. Many happy reunions took place when youngsters found their beloved cats. Many a stray tear was brushed aside by their happy parents. Others who came to the shelter to find a lost pet went away sad, realising that their beloved cat hadn't been so lucky with her nine lives.

Within three months the number of pets housed on Fox Hill had dropped from 2,000 to 200. Like all SPCA shelters that in Luzerne County is supported by sales at a thrift shop in the centre of population. This was destroyed in the flood. Also most of the dog banks placed in stores and restaurants were either lost or looted during the emergency.

One of the shelter's trucks happened to be in a garage for repair at the time the flood came and was lost.

Since the flood one of the local radio stations has turned over to the shelter $3,000 raised by its appeals.

Richard Evans, Sr, owner of this station has as the station mascot a cat who was rescued by the SPCA several years ago. Spike, as he is called, has been personalised by all the station personnel and continues to ask for help for the wonderful place that took care of his friends during the emergency.

'So many wonderful people have sent gifts,' says Miss Jones. 'We could never have gotten through the emergency without help, and we are most grateful.'

'Cats especially seem grateful for what has been done for them. They seem to actually beg for someone to comfort them, assure them that they are safe.'

This is just what happened to over a thousand cats that owe their lives to Miss Jones and her courageous helpers at the SPCA Humane Animal Shelter on Fox Hill in Wilkes Barre, Pennsylvania.

To the mariner, cattail is the inner part of a cathead which laps under the forecastle beams. In the mills of Lancashire it is a tuft of cotton that becomes cordlike and stringy owing to bad adjustment of the machinery. The cat-o'-nine tails (also called thief's cat) was that flogging rope dreaded by soldiers and sailors of other days. It was made of nine pieces of cord, each with three knots, attached to a thick rope handle. Everyone knows the cattails of marsh and border, but to a Canadian farmer cattail might also be a form of cirrus cloud.

GILEAN DOUGLAS, *Cats in our language*

The Cat Fancy past and present

KIT WILSON

Few people have not heard of the Kennel Club, but it is probably little known that there is a Cat Fancy which has been in existence since the 1880s. In those days it was vastly different from what it is today, but one can glean a lot of information about it from an interesting little paper called *Our Cats* published weekly price 1d and from Frances Simpson's *Book of the Cat*, now out of print and very difficult to come by. The Fancy in those days was small and would appear to have been a pleasant hobby for the rich—it counted among its members a princess or two and several ladies of title. Cat shows too seem to have been glorified social gatherings. Photos in fact show the exhibits being brought to the show either in open wagonettes or in the more humble 'growler' by members of the household staff both male and female. Some of the former were shown penning the cats in cap and apron! Later on in the day proud owners arrived in a carriage and pair, the coachman being accompanied by a little 'tiger' whose function was to carry cushions, rugs, and the luncheon basket, the contents of which was served by either the maid or the footman—hence the livery! Gentlemen too often graced the shows, always correctly dressed in morning attire complete with top hat and gloves. We read about judges but how they reached this exalted rank is not explained—nor indeed to what standard they judged, as at that time there were no standards of points. Never let it be said that the poor were forgotten; every Christmas the Fancy gave a dinner to the London catsmeat men at a long-since-forgotten hotel. The menu consisted of Brown Windsor soup, roast and two veg. and either pie or suet pudding with custard. And beer! These functions were always adorned by one or two of the gentlemen of the Fancy who welcomed the guests with a few well-chosen words, to which reply was made by the chief catsmeat man. One would suppose that he was selected by his fellows as we are not given any information about him in the paper. The gentlemen gracing the party did not dine with their guests but we are told that a good time was had by all.

Cats at that time had most noble names. Among them we find the Shah of Persia (a chinchilla), the Duke of Wellington (a tabby) and Lord Percy an angora—now called a white. These names made rather peculiar reading in the advertisement columns. For instance we find that Mrs X has reduced the stud fee of the Shah to 25s in order to make him available to all. In an announcement of the wedding between two members of the Fancy the writer hopes that Lord Percy will not be too distressed at being banned from the nuptial couch! Another astounding announcement in the personal column states that Mrs Y has had the misfortune to fall and hurt her arm, which must be kept in a sling, so she wishes it to be known that she will not be mating for about three months! In *Cat Chat* we read of a most unfortunate occurrence at Devonshire House while the cats were being paraded on collars and leads. Miss M's big black male broke his ribbon lead and fiercely attacked his neighbour, a beautiful blue with silver trimmings. The combat was noisy, the general row being added to by the screams of the ladies watching the parade, and was so great that one lady fainted. Meanwhile the black had taken refuge under the piano, whereupon Dr S showed the greatest of courage in recapturing the cat and got very badly scratched for his pains. One lovely photo is of a show held at the Botanical Gardens, in a marquee, the gentlemen judges resplendent in white flannels, bright cricket blazers, and straw boaters, while the lady judge is in muslin with a picture hat, her dress being finished off with a train.

At the turn of the century a few cat clubs had been formed, the chief of these being the National Cat Club, which issued licences for shows, registered cats and acted as a governing body. But the serpent had to enter this Eden and some members fell out among themselves, meetings were called and, as one writer of the day remarked, there was a great deal of talk as usual and people were most insulting to one another. The end was a breakaway and the formation of The Cat Club.

This body too acted as registrars, and licensed shows. Exhibitors could show at either but to do so had to be registered with both, which caused great confusion. This continued until 1910 when that great cat artist, Louis Wain, tried to pour oil on troubled waters. He called a meeting of all the Cat Fancy, pointed out the Gilbertian situation they had got themselves into and suggested a compromise: there should be one governing body, to which clubs could be affiliated, ruled by delegates from each such affiliated club. In this he was supported by the moderates from both the National and the Cat Club, but the latter body was unable to accept and walked out. In spite of this other clubs agreed and thus the Governing Council of the Cat Fancy was born, the National ceding rights as registrar and licensee to the Council which in return gave the National the right of having four delegates to the Council in perpetuity. The Council flourished and gradually the Cat Club folded up and peace reigned. But not for long, four years after the formation of the GC the 1914 war broke out, catteries were disbanded and cat breeding ceased.

In 1920 it started up again, Some of the old members were still with it, but gone were the days of maids in streamers. Exhibitors arrived in motor cars, or by bus, the elderly ladies having with them little messsenger boys, who arrived at the show hall in charge of an officer and waited to be hired!

The great show of the season was the National held at the Crystal Palace for two days. Judges now wore white coats and had a standard of points for every variety. Each judge was accompanied by one or more stewards, also clad in white coats. In those days stewards had to show great respect for their judges, do what they were told and not speak unless spoken to. Even at lunch (provided by the Club) judges had the high table while stewards sat below.

The spirit of competition was entering the Fancy—not always

the right spirit. At one Palace show an exhibitor was disciplined for tipping a box of white powder over a black cat. This brought about the rule that powder is banned from the show hall, a rule which exists today. Another semi-riot was caused by some exhibitors who were aggrieved over something, advancing in a body on the show manager, who took refuge behind the piles of chairs in the concert hall and only emerged when the disturbance was quelled by the attendants!

The Fancy, however, was on an upward trend and things in general were much more professional—not that they did not have their funny side. One judge always wore her hat while judging. One of these had a peacock's feather in front and as she bent down to look at the exhibits this flapped about and all down the line paws were put through the bars in an endeavour to catch it.

The most outstanding memory of these shows at the Crystal Palace took place when, 48 hours before the show was to open, the old Palace was burnt to the ground. The show manager that year was Mrs Sharman. Undaunted she set to work and found another hall (they were easier to get in those days). Luckily the pens had not been erected, so they were able to go straight over. Judges and exhibitors were notified, either by wire or telephone, and the show went on as usual. A masterly piece of showmanship.

The Second World War boded ill for the Fancy. Many cats were put to sleep, catteries were disbanded and some of the best cats left the country for ever but it never quite died. The chairman of the Governing Council, the late Cyril Yeates, kept in touch with those he was able to and little meetings took place to keep things alive, so that when peace came a start could be made again. A great effort was made by the Nottingham and Derby Cat Club who under almost insuperable difficulties staged the first post-war show. Gradually other clubs followed but it took a considerable time to get things really going. Today the Fancy flourishes. Not only has the wind of change blown over it but it has experienced a virtual gale: no longer are shows a miniature Ascot, gone are the elegant ladies and the top-hatted gentlemen. Today shorthaired girls and long-haired boys call 'across the crowded room'. Judges and stewards are mostly on Christian-name terms and the knowledge of cats is very great. In many ways the change has been all for the good but in some particular ways it has been the reverse. No longer is it a delightful hobby—though show me the person who keeps cats properly and makes money—but there are those to whom cat breeding is commerce. These are chiefly backyard breeders who keep their cats in bad conditions, using them like machines and disposing of them when they are of no further value. These people regard their cats and kittens solely as a cheque on four legs and, while the Fancy does what it can to drive them out, there is little it can do.

Type in cats has altered very considerably and there are some really magnificent specimens on the bench today. In some varieties the trend towards experimental breeding, i.e. mixing varieties and colours to produce an exotic cat such as the Havana and the Foreign white, has caused some deterioration among the original stock— chiefly in the Siamese and British shorthair.

Cat shows, which used to be held only in the months between September and February, are now held throughout the year and, as more and more clubs are formed, so more and more shows are applied for and in many cases they have to overlap. In the old days the secretary to the Council was also the registrar; today there are five more registrars, registrations run into thousands and so large are the shows that anything up to 80 judges have to be engaged—as at the National. Besides the Governing Council the running of the Fancy is by the executive committee which meets monthly—as against the quarterly meetings of the Council. Other committees are the disciplinary, the finance, and the genetics. These meet whenever necessary.

Delegates to the General Council are elected by their clubs, but the executive council is elected from the delegates at the June meeting. At this meeting the chairman of the Council is elected by the delegates, annually, but there is a limit of three years to his term of office.

The humble moggy of the nineteenth century has now evolved into the aristocrat of today and the social gatherings of the turn of the century have now evolved into a Fancy open to all, irrespective of creed, race or class, who are interested in that lovable furry animal the cat.

If you are thinking of joining, a word of warning. To keep cats healthy is expensive so do not expect to become wealthy. Be wise, and you'll get lots of fun and make many friends.

Cat shows of yesteryear and today

GRACE POND FZS

The day that saw the birth of the Cat Fancy throughout the world was 16 July 1871—although no one realised it at the time. The first dog show had been held more than a decade before, but the idea of exhibiting cats in such a way was an entirely new one. They had appeared as side shows at agricultural and county shows, even at circuses but, until Harrison Weir organised the show at the Crystal Palace, no one considered there would be much interest in a show devoted entirely to cats.

Harrison Weir was a most versatile and clever man. As well as designing the cups for the winning horses at Ascot and Goodwood, he judged at poultry and pigeon shows. He wrote a comprehensive book on poultry, was a skilful artist and was also a Fellow of the Royal Horticultural Society. His book *Our Cats and all about them*, published in 1889, was the first to set out standards—which he called 'points of excellence'—by which cats could be judged.

He decided to hold a cat show 'so that the different breeds, colours, markings, etc. might be more carefully attended to, and the domestic cat, sitting in front of the fire would then possess a beauty and attractiveness to its owner unobserved and unknown because uncultivated heretofore.' His idea was criticised by many and treated with ridicule by others but the great success of the venture soon silenced the critics.

The first show attracted an entry of about 170 cats and kittens, mostly shorthairs. According to *The Graphic* of 22 July 1871, the entries included

> Siamese cats, quite new to the country . . . soft fawn-coloured creatures, with jet-black legs—an unnatural nightmare kind of cat. . . . A French African cat, a very beautiful creature, with long woolly hair of a light brown colour. A Persian, direct from Persia, remarkable for the great beauty of his black, grey and white coat . . . a very amiable beast. An enormous English cat, weighing 21 pounds. His colour was a rich brown ground, striped with black. A native of the Isle of Man, with the usual Manx absence of tail. This cat takes to the water like a dog and catches fish.

A British wildcat which had lost his right front paw was also exhibited. 'He behaved like a mad devil, and ten men could not get him into a wire cage out of the box in which he was sent.'

The prize winners included a white Persian, with dark blue eyes and the prize for the fattest cat went to one weighing over 20 pounds. There was also a tortoiseshell tom which attracted a great deal of attention, as tortoiseshells are invariably female. It was said of him that he was 'poor in colour and very feminine in appearance'.

The show had 25 classes with the cats being entered mainly according to colour. The entry fee for each class was 3/6d, with £70 being offered in prize money. One shilling was charged for admission which was quite expensive for those days but so many visitors turned up that at times it proved well-nigh impossible to even see a cat. At the end of the show, Harrison Weir was presented with a pint-sized silver tankard by the Crystal Palace Company 'in recognition of his suggestions and services'. Such was the success of the show that another was arranged for the December of the same year.

By 1873 shows were being held at the Alexandra Palace, London, and in Birmingham as well as at the Crystal Palace. Scotland, too, took up cats with enthusiasm, the 1875 show in Edinburgh having the astonishing entry of 560 cats. Special exhibits included a 'fireman's cat' which had been rescued by a fireman from the ninth storey of a burning house and a 'cabman's cat', rescued after being locked in an empty house by a family which had moved away. One lady was so impressed by his kind act that she presented the cabman with a shelter for his cab rank.

At the 1873 Crystal Palace show an innovation was a class for 'Wild or Hybrid between Wild and Domestic cats'. The winner was a beautiful ocelot but there is no mention of how it was judged.

Cats became the fashion, shows being patronised by no less personages than Queen Victoria—who owned two blue Persians—and the Prince of Wales, later Edward VII, who personally presented photographs of himself to the owners of prize-winning cats. In no time at all cats had almost become early status symbols and the committees of early clubs included such names as Lady Decies, Lady Alexander and the Hon. Mrs McLaren Morrison among others.

Following the success of cat shows in Britain, America followed suit and the first large show was held there in 1895 at Madison Square Gardens in New York. Mr James H. Hyde was the organiser, the show being run on the same lines as the Crystal Palace shows. Cats were imported from Britain to found new catteries and it is still possible to trace some pedigrees right back to those early days.

By 1889 the Crystal Palace show was attracting an entry of nearly 600 cats and kittens, with more than 19,000 people paying to see the exhibits. This was the age of elegance in the cat world, with exhibitors dressing as if for a fashion rather than a cat show. They may be seen in old photographs wearing long flowing dresses and enormous picture hats. There was no question of the lady judges wearing white overalls—their dress had to be gracious and elaborate.

Large catteries abounded. Domestic help was easy to come by and many famous owners had staff who spent their time looking after, grooming and feeding the cats. Lady Marcus Beresford was said to have had about 160 cats at one time, whose names, not surprisingly, featured constantly among the winners. She was in a position to travel all over the country, with her retinue, exhibiting at various shows, sometimes, according to old catalogues, entering more than 30 cats at a single show.

Some fanciers were so bitten by the show bug and were so keen to win that, if a cat they owned was beaten, every endeavour was made to buy the victor no matter what the price, to ensure that it would not again compete against the exhibit they were anxious to make a champion.

Harrison Weir judged at the first show according to his 'points of excellence'. His fellow judges were his brother, John Jenner Weir, and the Rev. J. Macdona. Other judges at the early shows were Dr Gordon Stables, who also wrote on cats, and a Mr P. H. Jones. In a year or two they were joined by Miss Frances Simpson, who wrote *The Book of the Cat* (Cassells, 1903) and bred a number of winning cats, including the first outstanding blue Persians. Mr C. A. House, who also wrote on cats, and Mr T. B. Mason, who bred and exhibited a number of varieties, were among the new judges. Although judges are not now permitted to exhibit and judge at the same show, Harrison Weir showed his blue tabby, The Old Lady, at the first show. She won a small silver bell of which he was very proud.

From the first, the pens and tabling were very much the same as used at the shows today but, instead of litter trays, earth or sawdust was placed in the back of the pen for the cat's toilet use and a cushion or straw or hay was put in front for the cat to sit on. Eucalyptus was recommended as a disinfectant and an RSPCA official was frequently in attendance to see that all was well with the cats when they were taken out of their baskets. Veterinary surgeons, as now, examined each exhibit before it was allowed to be penned but unfortunately infection was rife. Inoculation was unknown and frequently whole catteries were wiped out after the return home of one exhibit from a show. This was due to feline infectious enteritis but poison was often suspected, as it was not realised that an illness could strike and kill so swiftly, with an animal sometimes dying within a matter of hours. It was not appreciated that infection could persist for months in a house and often a new kitten, bought to replace one that had died, fell a victim itself within a few days. The pens at the shows too were used over and over again and the death rate after a show was terrible. Eventually some fanciers refused to exhibit. Advertisements appeared in cat magazines stating that the advertiser had some very attractive kittens for sale but was not exhibiting them because of the great risk involved. Other fanciers gave up breeding altogether, preferring to have the cats neutered and kept entirely as pets. A Mrs G. H. Walker had an excellent cattery where she bred chinchillas and, even judging by today's standards, hygiene and cleanliness were the first consideration but, according to an early writer, ' Such losses as

Mrs Walker sustained were enough to damp the ardour of the most enthusiastic cat lover and fancier; but the lady . . . bravely faced the situation, and after a period of sad reflection she once again resumed her hobby with renewed interest.'

As well as the cats being judged by their pens, as is the British custom still, there were also ring classes at some shows similar to those at dog shows with cats being drawn (or dragged) around the ring by brightly coloured ribbons by very elegantly dressed owners. One judge of that time, Miss Frances Simpson, deplored these classes and said 'It is quite absurd to mix up the sexes and dangerous to allow tom cats to come within fighting distance of each other.' One can imagine the scene at one show, where according to her, 'great excitement was caused in the ring by the sudden attack of one famous stud cat on another, with one 'sustaining a torn and bleeding ear'. Eventually to everyone's relief the class was dropped from the show schedules.

In Britain for many years—indeed up to the beginning of the Second World War—it was possible to send cats to a show unaccompanied and show managers had to arrange for their collection at the various London termini. These cats had to be penned, often groomed, fed and generally looked after and then returned the same way as they had come. Now it is a strict rule that all exhibits must be taken to a show by the owner or a representative. This is certainly one headache less for the over-worked show manager.

As more shows were held throughout the country, the numbers of pedigree cats increased. At first, of course, none of the cats had pedigrees and little was understood about the possibilities for breeding for certain colours but gradually more varieties were produced. The rapid expansion of the British Cat Fancy practically came to a standstill with the 1914–18 war and at the first show afterwards, held in 1920, only 236 cats were entered. The numbers crept up gradually but once again received a severe set-back with the Second World War. Catteries were dispersed, animals were put to sleep or neutered and breeding practically ceased. Some well-known breeders managed to keep a few cats and were instrumental in starting the Fancy going once again. At the National Cat Club show held in 1947 there were only 200 entries. It is incredible to think that at the club's centenary show in 1971 there were nearly 2,000 cats and kittens exhibited.

Not all the drop in numbers could be blamed on the wars alone.

In some cases it was due to very violent outbreaks of feline infectious enteritis—one such outbreak which occurred in the early 1920s resulted in the death of thousands of cats. The introduction of suitable vaccines and the consequent saving of life after the Second World War has proved the saving grace of the Cat Fancy, with most breeders having their kittens inoculated as soon as old enough.

Over the years, by selective breeding and deeper understanding as to how different colours and coat patterns could be produced, the number of varieties gradually increased, until now more than 50 have been produced and recognised. Consequently the size of the shows is also ever increasing.

Cat shows are now held all over the British Isles. They fall into three categories. Firstly there are the championship shows in which challenge certificates are granted. The winning of three such certificates under three different judges at three shows means the cat may become a champion. Secondly come sanction shows which are really dress rehearsals by clubs which hope eventually to put on championship shows—but no challenge certificates are given. Lastly there are exemption shows, small shows held in local halls with as few as 60 cats entered. The rules are not so stringent as in the previous two. All these shows are held under the sponsorship of the Governing Council of the Cat Fancy who impose strict regulations regarding their organisation.

The most recent highlights of the Cat Fancy was the largest cat show ever to be held in the world. It was the National Cat Club Show of 1971—a hundred years after the first Crystal Palace show. Nearly 2,000 cats and kittens were entered and these were judged by judges from various overseas countries as well as more than 80 British judges. Congratulations were received from many other Cat Fancies and, most important of all, there was a congratulatory letter from HM Queen Elizabeth II.

Unless something unforeseen happens, pedigree cats and the numbers at cat shows should always increase. After all, they are the shop windows of the Cat Fancy. Shows not only enable breeders to exhibit their stock and by their wins to ascertain their quality, they also become well known for their cats and can then sell them. The general public too are able to visit the shows and to see for themselves the charm and elegance of these cats which, according to Harrison Weir before he started all this 'show business', were 'unobserved and unknown' only 100 years ago.